East Meets West

East Meets West

The stories of the remarkable men and women from
the East and the West who built a bridge across
a cultural divide and introduced Meditation
and Eastern Philosophy to the West

John Adago

SHEPHEARD-WALWYN (PUBLISHERS) LTD

:

First published in 2014 by
Shepheard-Walwyn (Publishers) Ltd
107 Parkway House, Sheen Lane,
London SW14 8LS
www.shepheard-walwyn.co.uk

British Library Cataloguing in Publication Data
A catalogue record of this book
is available from the British Library

ISBN: 978-0-85683-286-4

Typeset by Alacrity, Chesterfield, Sandford, Somerset
Printed in the USA
by Edwards Brothers Inc

*He was a teacher of philosophy and
a Socratic scholar who lived
the philosophy he taught.*

*This history is dedicated to
Frederick Helmers
and all who knew him.*

To Roy & Dianne

We walked This path Toward
Truth & Self Discovery
for many years
I wish you well

Yal Arley

Contents

Photographs

Acknowledgements

I WANT TO THANK the many who took the time to help with editing, correcting, and encouragement. Among them, my wife Catherine, Shirley Burch, Norbert Chusid, Harley Dembert, Elena Fong, Carlo Frua, Cedric Grigg, Margaret Hooper, Ed Kinslow, Barbara McLaughin, Toinette Lippe, Gary Shelton, Paul Shepherd, John Stewart, Clark Stillman, Joseph Sundwall, Dorine Tolley, and Christopher Urban.

Thank you Joy Dillingham for inspiration and encouragement, and to my publisher Anthony Werner for shaping a manuscript into the finished book.

Thanks to the Yale Library for making available the Centennial Collection of the Complete Works of P.D. Ouspensky, and a special acknowledgement for the work of Bill Hager and the Study Society for preserving and making available the words of Shantananda Saraswati and Dr Francis C. Roles. And to Donald and Christine Lambie, who have been sources of knowledge and inspiration to so many.

Introduction

 EAST MEETS WEST is a phrase often heard and a story seldom told. This is the history of the introduction of meditation and Eastern philosophy to Western Civilization. Today meditation is practiced by millions of people throughout the West, and has become a household word. Virtually every religion has revived a form of the practice; it is taught in schools, business seminars and has been the subject of scientific research. Fifty years ago it was little known, it was considered an obscure practice, 'contemplating one's navel', or something a hermit did in a cave that had little relevance to Europeans and Americans engaged in worldly pursuits. This practice, little known in the West, became widespread in less than fifty years through the work of 'The Teachers', the men and women who built a bridge across a cultural divide and transmitted the knowledge of an ancient tradition to the West. These remarkable men and women devoted their lives to the search for truth and higher knowledge, and to making it available to others. They lived by the principle of 'Learn and teach'. This work became the aim and purpose of their life. Their lives are a source of inspiration and provide an example of the perseverance, devotion, and commitment needed if one is to 'Work on Oneself' with the aim of reaching one's highest potential. They lived their lives on a world stage, and they played their parts well. It would not be possible to include every member of the cast; the intent here is to tell the story of some of the major players.

For students of Eastern philosophy, those who meditate, and those who engage in 'The Work', this history is their heritage.

Many of the facts and quotes have been gathered from the author's conversations with Joy Dillingham, Leon MacLaren, Nicolai Rabeneck, William Hager, Sitaram Jaiswal, Willem Nyland, Swami Muktananda, and from transcripts of conversations with Gurdjieff, Ouspensky, Willem Nyland, Gurudeva, Dr Roles, Leon MacLaren, and Shantananda Saraswati. Additional sources have been footnoted and listed in the bibliography.

The science and technology that shaped Western Civilization began with the classical scientists. In the middle of the second millennium there was an awakening in Europe. It started as an inquiry into the nature of the world in which we live. Copernicus, Kepler, and Newton observed the planets and began investigating the laws that governed their movements. The men of knowledge in Europe sought to understand matter and energy. Darwin expounded a theory of the origin of species, as engineers, digging canals in Europe, discovered a recorded history of the planet in the layers of the earth. These inquiries led to a mastery of metallurgy, thermodynamics, electrical, and nuclear power. During our lifetime worldwide communication has become instantaneous, and distances between continents are traversed in hours.

In the East, the inquiry was governed by ancient tradition. Although the first experiments in printing, gunpowder, and metallurgy were begun in the East, they did not evolve as they did in Europe. Scientific research and exploration were of more interest to the West than to the East. The interest of the Brahmins was of a different nature from that of the learned men of Europe. The exploration in the East was in the Spiritual Sciences. The West sought mastery over matter; the East sought Self-mastery. The West strove for freedom from want and poverty; the East sought freedom from desire and suffering. While scientists in the West investigated the principles and laws that govern nature, the learned men of the East sought to lift the veil of illusion that kept men from reaching their highest potential.

1

Seekers of Truth

WITH THE OPENING of the trade routes and the beginning of commerce, there began a transmission of knowledge and technology from the West to the East. The transmission of the spiritual philosophy from East to West is a more recent story – a story largely untold. It began in Armenia at the crossroads of the trade routes. In the first years of the twentieth century a small group came together who called themselves, 'Seekers of Truth'. This group of fifteen men, and one woman, had among them scientists, explorers, an anthropologist, a medical doctor, a linguist, a priest, a wealthy prince, who funded many of their expeditions, and one man with an indomitable will, George I. Gurdjieff.

Gurdjieff was born in Alexandropol, a city in Armenia, now called Gyumri, in 1876. His mother was Armenian. His father, Ivan, of Greek stock, was widely known as one of the last of the bards with a remarkable memory who recited epic poems, legends, and myths. Through this oral tradition, history, legend, and folklore were passed down from one generation to another. Gurdjieff once read an article that described the discovery of tablets in ancient Babylon that were four thousand years old. The article printed the inscription and the translation of an ancient legend he had often heard his father recite. To his astonishment the words he read matched in word and form the poem his father recited; it had been passed down unchanged for four thousand years![1]

His father, seeking to prepare him for the priesthood, arranged for his son to receive an exceptional education. Gurdjieff's mentor, Father Borsh, was the dean of Kars Military Cathedral. He was a physician and the spiritual authority for the region. As Gurdjieff's tutor, he guided him in his studies of theology and medicine. It was his belief that in order to attend to the needs of the body or the spirit one needed knowledge of both.[2]

The group of seekers shared a belief that there existed ancient knowledge that had been forgotten by all but a few. They investigated the traditional sources of science, religion, and philosophy, and what they found convinced them that there was a profound and complete body of knowledge, known to a few, that could guide men and women to fulfill what they believed was the highest purpose of human life.

They began to make expeditions, 'journeys to inaccessible places', to remote regions of Egypt, Persia, Tibet, and India, in search of a teacher, a monastery, a brotherhood – repositories where ancient knowledge had been passed down from generation to generation by way of teacher to disciple.

By this tradition, an aspirant seeks out a master teacher to whom he makes a commitment. The student studies and works under the guidance and discipline of the teacher who prepares him not simply to hear knowledge, but to strengthen his ability to reason and cleanse his heart so that true understanding can be achieved. After years of preparation the student begins to realize the knowledge of the master within himself. Eventually the student becomes the master and takes on the next generation of students.

The group undertook difficult journeys to remote regions lasting months, sometimes more than a year. They traveled vast distances on foot with pack animals, overcoming difficult terrain, hostile local people, and diseases. Not all survived, not all returned, yet some found the knowledge for which they were searching. Prince Yuri Lubovedsky, who had been one of the seekers from the beginning, stayed at a brotherhood that was one of their destinations for the remainder of his life.[3]

Gurdjieff said little about his sources of knowledge: secrecy may well have been a condition of gaining access to these inner circles. He mentions a monastery on Mount Athos with a lineage reaching back to 500 BC, a brotherhood with a lineage to the early Christians, and a school in Chinese Turkistan. Many of the areas that he traveled through were soon after devastated by war. The knowledge he brought to the West may have been all that survived from these esoteric groups. In *All and Everything,* he wrote that one of the great tragedies of war was the destruction of institutions, records, and traditions that preserved knowledge.

He encountered master teachers of several traditions, and he was influenced by the Sufis and the Dervishes. In India he met teachers on the way of knowledge, the way of devotion, and the way of the fakir (physical discipline). These were traditions known only to a few, and these disciplines were referred to as the three Paths or Ways to Spiritual Development.

He returned to the West with a profound understanding of the nature of Man, his place in the cosmos, and the laws that governed him. He also brought back knowledge of the methods by which men and women could work toward an inner transformation and expanded awareness. He called his method 'The Fourth Way', for it incorporated elements of the three ways of knowledge, devotion, and physical discipline. This was practiced not in the seclusion of a monastery or hermitage but while carrying on the life of a house-holder, fulfilling the responsibilities of family, profession, and citizen.

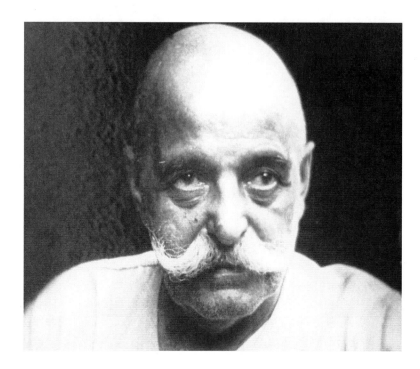

GEORGE IVANOVITCH GURDJIEFF
(1876-1949)

To possess the right to the name Man, one must be one. He must with an indefatigable persistence and an unquenchable desire, issuing from one's entirety, that is to say, from thought, feeling and organic instinct, work on all-round knowledge of oneself – at the same time: struggling unceasingly with one's subjective weaknesses, striving for their eradication without mercy towards oneself.*

He must strive:

1 To have everything necessary for his physical well being.
2 For self-perfection.
3 To know ever more about the laws of world creation and world maintenance.
4 To pay for the cause of his arising as quickly as possible, so as to be free to lighten the Sorrow of Our Common Father.
5 To assist others in their work toward self-perfection.†

Adapted from *All and Everything*: *p.1209, † p.386.
Photo taken by Dushka Howarth, France, 1949 – the year of his death.

2

Gurdjieff in Russia

I T WAS 1912 when Gurdjieff, first appeared in Moscow and St Petersburg. Though not a large man, his presence was commanding, and he had piercing eyes set in a round face. Rather like Socrates, who taught mainly in public spaces, Gurdjieff sat most afternoons in the sidewalk cafes where he attracted a circle of interested people. One alert observer described him as a man 'poorly disguised as ordinary'. He was something more than what was conveyed by his dress and mannerisms. He stood out simply because his actions and speech proceeded with apparent indifference to the opinions of those around him. His reference point was within himself. He was a man with an aim and a purpose. He sought to realize within himself the knowledge that had taken many years to acquire. His will did not waiver and he was not subject to the distractions that govern the lives of most men. 'Those who followed Gurdjieff never doubted that he always said what he did for a reason, that he was tireless and never forgot his aim; in their opinion he was always teaching, and for them he was.'[1] He sought to attract men and women in whom he could cultivate the seeds of Eastern knowledge and thereby introduce the wisdom of the East to Western Europe.

Some masters teach through lucid discourse, some inspire devotion, some by manifesting strength, courage, and acts of daring. Gurdjieff used all these methods, but mainly he affected a change in his students by the sheer power of his will. P.D. Ouspensky (see Chapter 3), writing in *In Search of the Miraculous,* described an inner conversation, without spoken words, during which Gurdjieff conveyed to him profound insights.[2] Leon MacLaren (see Chapter 7) told me Gurdjieff had developed extraordinary powers. In his writings he mentions healing and the ability to facilitate the cure of people with serious addictions. He also mentioned that he could generate a force that could kill a yak.[3] At times, to continue his work; he organized businesses and earned large sums of money even in the most adverse of circumstances. Many of his students wrote that he was able to affect a profound change in those who chose to come under his influence. Through elucidation, reason, guidance, confrontation, and intimidation, he motivated people to strive to liberate themselves from the habits and superficial concerns governing their lives.

Gurdjieff's description of mankind was not flattering. Being aware that men and women have the potential to develop reason and the capacity for wisdom and higher emotions – compassion, empathy, and universal love, he recognized that in their ordinary state they rarely manifest any of these.

He called them 'machines' whose habitual reactions to impressions and circumstances were little more than knee-jerk responses acquired during their formative years and reinforced by repetition. They had little will and a fleeting attention span that would miss the opportunity of the moment. They were often preoccupied: reliving the past, ruminating about some future possibility, or simply in a daydream. He described the level of consciousness in which men and women live most of their lives as a 'waking sleep'. He said that although mankind has the capacity for reason and a higher level of awareness, the forces of nature work against that potential in the great mass of humanity. As part of organic life on earth, mankind served as transforming machines, absorbing oxygen, carbohydrates, impressions of light and sound, and then transforming them mechanically and involuntarily into carbon dioxide, nitrates, and incessant thoughts and superficial feelings such as worry, jealousy, vanity, etc. Men and women were subject to daydreaming and distorting imagination, as well as plagued by incessant inner conversations and repeating circular thoughts. 'Man is a machine. All his deeds, words, thoughts, feelings, convictions, opinions, and habits are the result of external influences, external impressions. Out of himself a man cannot produce a single thought, a single action. Everything he does, thinks, feels – all this happens.'[4]

He said the forces of nature bound most of mankind to a life that was often unbecoming of beings with the potential for reason, wisdom, and the noblest of human emotions. But this was not the fate of all mankind. In every generation some could liberate themselves from the 'human condition', acquire knowledge and work to transform themselves. In fact, it was critical that a certain number do so to provide a harmonizing influence, a conscious impulse, to balance the irrational tendencies of the masses.[5] He warned that humanity had entered a precarious period: *'Unless the wisdom of the East and the energy of the West are harnessed and used harmoniously the world will destroy itself.'*[6]

This evolution of consciousness is not natural. It does not occur as a result of life experience alone. It requires an active participation, a conscious effort, and special knowledge not generally available. He would say to people, 'I cannot develop you … I can only create conditions in which you can develop yourself … Take the understanding of the East and the energy of the West and then seek!'[7] Gurdjieff called this 'The Work'. He taught a process of impartial self-observation to raise the level of consciousness so that people might come out from under the spell of daydreams, conceits and vanities, and acquire the knowledge to transform themselves, unify the will, enhance the power of attention, and expand awareness.

His groups were growing during the turbulent years preceding World War I and the chaos of the Russian Revolution. Conditions were so uncertain that they awoke some mornings not knowing which political faction was in power. Even with this political and economic instability, Gurdjieff continued to teach and to attract students. The intense interest of those attracted to Gurdjieff's work reflected the fervor of a world preparing for the most destructive war to afflict humanity, which would claim eight million lives (Worse was to follow when World War II claimed fifty million lives).

One of those attracted to Gurdjieff, a journalist named Pyotr D. Ouspensky, observed stockpiles of crutches and stretchers being made for limbs not yet lost in a war not yet begun, and was struck by man's blind irrationality. Gurdjieff referred to war as 'a period of reciprocal mass destruction'. These were times when men destroyed each other, as well as the families, institutions, and traditions that upheld civilization. He believed the greatest tragedy was the loss of the knowledge embodied in these institutions and traditions. These periods were beyond man's power to control because certain alignments of planets created a tension in the psyche of mankind. This inner tension drove the masses into periods of war and civil unrest. However, for a few, who came under guidance and knowledge, this same tension manifested as a desire to overcome one's limitations and aspire to one's highest potential.[8]

Gurdjieff organized entertainments performed in theaters in St Petersburg and Moscow to attract attention and generate interest in his ideas. In later years these demonstrations were performed in Paris, London, and in the United States. These were unusual spectacles: dances and sacred movements that embodied esoteric laws and universal principles that were taught to students who performed them to music. These sacred dances and religious rituals, which Gurdjieff and the 'Seekers' discovered, had been preserved in certain temples and monasteries in Tibet, Turkistan, Persia, and other places. These dances and movements have always been one of the subjects taught in esoteric schools in the East. They serve a dual purpose: to convey knowledge of laws and principles and to be a means of bringing about a balance and harmony within the participants.

Some of the performances included demonstrations of Gurdjieff's extraordinary powers and a mixture of tricks and illusions. Audiences were left to make sense of what they had witnessed. This was in keeping with Gurdjieff's enigmatic nature. On one evening one might see a profound philosopher, on another, a provocative and unorthodox teacher who created conditions for students that shook their psychological foundations and challenged their core beliefs.

When conditions in Russia grew too unstable to continue, Gurdjieff moved the center of his work. In 1922 he set up the Institute for the Harmonious Development of Man at Fontainebleau in France. In this country estate students stepped away from their habitual routines. Gurdjieff had them engage in gardening, property maintenance, construction, meal preparation, and other physical work.

Students often worked with others with whom they had little in common except their interest in the Work. They were often in groups with others of different nationality and social class. Some of the frictions and interactions led to humorous moments. On one occasion four West Europeans complained to Gurdjieff about a Russian they found to be obnoxious. After describing some of his offensive behavior, one exasperated Frenchman asked Gurdjieff if he could get rid of him. 'Yes, I can get rid of him', Gurdjieff replied, 'but then I would have to find someone to replace him'.

These activities and the interaction with each other, as well as the movements class and special exercises, gave students an opportunity to observe their actions and habits, as well as their ideas and thoughts. These practices provided glimpses of their limitations and a deeper understanding of their essential nature. Under Gurdjieff's direction, conditions were set up to heighten awareness and to actualize the principles he was teaching. The programs students engaged in were intense. The Work entailed observation, self-examination, and a striving to become free of habitual thoughts, feelings, and actions, which cut people off from their essential nature. Gurdjieff taught as much by action as by words. He once invited students to his flat in Paris for a dinner party. They arrived to find Gurdjieff had spent days preparing exotic dishes and delicacies from many of the regions to which he had traveled. The guests enjoyed the elaborate feast, though some grew 'self-conscious' when they realized that throughout the evening Gurdjieff ate and drank nothing.

Gurdjieff's near-fatal car accident in 1924 brought The Institute to an abrupt end. But the methods he taught had far reaching affects. Willem Nyland, John G. Bennett, Thomas De Hartman, Mme de Salzmann, and Mme Ouspensky were among those who learned and later taught the methods of the Institute. During Gurdjieff's long convalescence his beautiful wife Ulosifna grew ill and died of cancer in 1926. He felt great remorse that, during her terminal illness, he himself was too weak to help her recover from a condition that he had successfully treated in others. As his strength returned he directed his attention to writing *All and Everything* and *Meetings with Remarkable Men*.

Gurdjieff lived another twenty-five years after recovering from his accident. In France, in 1949, on the last day of his life he was attended by a young American, Dr William Welch, who left his bedside, stepped into the adjoining room and told an anxious group the end was near. A few minutes later, Gurdjieff, with great effort, got up and moved his body across the room to the bathroom and then returned unassisted to his bed. It appeared to the doctor that he had lifted his failed body, as if by the scruff of his neck, and directed it to walk.[9] The teacher had given his last lesson; it was not the body that set the limits of a man, it was his will. His final act demonstrated the indomitable will that had manifested during his entire life.

As Gurdjieff had directed, his funeral was held at the Russian Orthodox Church in the Rue Daru. The priest read a prepared eulogy that ended with a quote from Gurdjieff's ballet, *The Struggle of the Magicians*, 'Lord Creator and all His assistants, help us to be able to remember ourselves at all times in order that we may avoid involuntary actions, as only through them can evil manifest itself.'[10]

During Gurdjieff's last year, despite increased infirmity due to illness, he called many of his students to him so that he might impart to them the essential experience of the Fourth Way. Dr Welch, who was by his bedside when he died, wrote: 'What can one learn from the death of a man who was truly a man? He had lived with the inevitability of his death as a daily reality to him, yet he had lived, if ever a man did, to the full. I have seen many men die, Gurdjieff died like a king.'[11]

PYOTR DEMIANOVICH OUSPENSKY
(1878-1947)

I went to India in search of a school or schools. I realized that personal or individual efforts were insufficient and it was necessary to come in touch with the real and living thought which must be in existence somewhere, but with which we had lost touch. I was going to 'seek the miraculous,' I had come to the conclusion that there was no escape from the labyrinth of contradictions in which we live our life except by an entirely new road.

The 'miraculous' was a penetration beneath the thin film of our superficial life to an unknown reality. And it seemed to me that the way to that reality could be found in the East.

Adapted from *In Search of the Miraculous*, pp.3-4.

3

P. D. Ouspensky

The Work Comes to London

IN 1915, one of Gurdjieff's exhibitions in Moscow attracted the attention of P.D. Ouspensky, a Russian author, journalist, and lecturer. Ouspensky had traveled to India and Egypt on his own search for esoteric knowledge. He was convinced that throughout history there had been 'Schools', seldom visible, that held, and at times made available, sacred knowledge. He believed such Schools had existed in ancient Greece and Italy, and in monasteries in Europe, which had inspired the Masons to build the great Gothic cathedrals, and that esoteric Schools had provided the impulse for the Renaissance in Europe. He also believed that such Schools still existed in India.

His study of mathematics had led him to seek an understanding of infinity and a multidimensional universe, and he had given a series of lectures on his travels and discoveries under the title, 'In Search of the Miraculous'.

The meeting between Gurdjieff and Ouspensky was auspicious. Ouspensky realized that Gurdjieff had found the esoteric knowledge for which he had been searching and recognized the importance of what Gurdjieff was imparting. He believed the power and intensity were of an order that could only have come from a level of understanding far higher than the ordinary. He had searched and worked for many years and was well prepared to receive what Gurdjieff had to teach. His experience and talents complemented those of Gurdjieff, who spoke many languages but was not fluent in the languages of Western Europe. Ouspensky had a remarkable memory – there was no note-taking during his meetings and conversations with Gurdjieff, but his records of the conversations, as well as the diagrams and tables, were detailed and exact. Ouspensky's credentials as author and lecturer gave him access to the intelligentsia of European society. This, of course, was crucial.

With the advent of the communist revolution in the fall of 1917, followed by the outbreak of civil war, conditions in Russia became intolerable. Ouspensky and his family suffered hardship, including cold, hunger, and typhoid, which left him detesting Bolshevism. He said, 'Communism is not a political party, it is a plague'.[1]

His own reputation was growing. In 1919 while Ouspensky was attempting to flee from Russia, *Tertium Organum* was translated into English. It was published and well received in both England and America. In it he explored the idea of a fourth dimension,* relating it to infinity and time.

'Things are linked together not by time but by an *inner connection*,[†] an inner relationship. And time cannot separate things which are inwardly close and follow one from another... Phenomena which appear to us totally unrelated may be seen by another wider consciousness as part of one whole. Side by side with our view of things, another view is possible, another method of perception, a new understanding that regards a phenomenon not as something isolated, but in conjunction with all the chains intersecting it.'[2]

Before leaving Russia he wrote *A New Model of the Universe,* which was published later.

In August of 1921, he moved to London, where he was introduced to London's aristocracy by Lady Rothermere, who was both

---

*He had published *The Fourth Dimension* in 1901. He had also studied the Tarot and Alchemy. His book on the Tarot was published after his death.
†Emphasis added.

a student and a patron of Ouspensky. She provided him with a meeting place in a studio on Circus Road, introduced him to T.S. Eliot, Aldous Huxley, and other literary figures, and liberally distributed copies of *Tertium Organum*. Ouspensky contributed articles to *The New Age*, a magazine edited by A.R. Orage. Orage introduced him to well-known journalists, Theosophists, and followers of Jung, and he entered an elite literary circle of authors and lecturers. He established a group called The Historico-Psychological Society, which later became known as The Study Society. The group was devoted to the investigation of the nature of consciousness and to making practical use of the insights gained from these investigations.

Drawing on the knowledge he had learned from Gurdjieff, in his writing and lecturing, Ouspensky set out a cohesive system that encompassed the atom, the cosmos, and man. He showed how the Law of Three related to the Christian doctrine of the Trinity and to the Vedantic principle of the three gunā or forces – rajas, tamas, and sattva; how a combination of these three forces, active, passive, and neutralizing, are present in every event and phenomenon in the universe; and how they are embodied in the three centers within man: intellect, heart, and instinct. He taught methods to bring them into balance and harmony. Man, he maintained, was 'third-force blind', rarely aware of the reconciling or neutralizing force that creates a harmonious relationship between the other two. Often considering only his own desire, and bound by conditioning, habit, and conflicting ideas, he lives a life far short of his potential. However, there is the possibility of escape from this bondage, but first he must realize his predicament and have a strong desire for liberation – 'In order to escape he must first realize he is in prison'.[3]

Then he will need knowledge, not generally available, and a group of people with whom to work. Little can be accomplished alone: only with a group or 'School', guided by higher knowledge, is inner transformation possible. The unity of things cannot be realized by the mind in its ordinary state of consciousness. A unity, a pattern, an all-embracing meaning can only be known or experienced in a state of consciousness quite different from the ordinary. Unity could only be realized by a mind which had itself become unified.

Ouspensky also wrote of the Law of Seven, evident in the musical octave and the color spectrum. He used the Law of Seven to elucidate man's place in the creation that included the atom, man, solar system, cosmos, and The Absolute. Transformation was governed by this law. Of particular importance were the intervals in the octave where effort and a conscious impulse were needed if one was to evolve and develop.[4]

Ouspensky came to prefer Gurdjieff's ideas over the man himself. He had great reverence for the knowledge he had acquired from Gurdjieff, but some of Gurdjieff's methods did not suit him.[5] Gurdjieff's approach was more practical and less theoretical, with an emphasis on the movements and exercises, whereas Ouspensky had little interest or aptitude for the movements. Gurdjieff related to some students in ways Ouspensky would not have. Gurdjieff often created difficult circumstances for students that required them to make efforts to overcome obstacles. Ouspensky did not approve of these methods.

Even so, he never criticized Gurdjieff, though, as his own reputation and following in London grew, he began to discourage contact between his students and Gurdjieff. Nevertheless, Ouspensky remained in contact with Gurdjieff until 1931 and had his approval to write about the Work.[6] Certainly Gurdjieff did not disapprove of Ouspensky's groups and on one visit to London addressed them through an interpreter. Ouspensky's successor, Dr Roles, wrote in *A Lasting Freedom* that he believed Gurdjieff intended them to work independently and deliberately made it difficult for Ouspensky to remain with him.[7]

Ouspensky was assisted by his wife, who continued to work with Gurdjieff. Under her direction an estate was set up at Lyne Place outside London. Over a hundred students would gather on the weekends. Madame Ouspensky took what she learned from

Gurdjieff at the Institute, including the movements, and helped bring to life the principles and knowledge her husband taught. She directed students through days of work under guidance that allowed students to go beyond theoretical knowledge and begin to gain an understanding of their true self.[8] This teaching method of 'work under guidance' at Lyne Place was carried on by Dr Roles, Leon MacLaren, and others.

Ouspensky's group in London attracted over a thousand students, and he and his wife gathered a following in America as well. Ouspensky referred to these groups as preparatory, fourth way Schools. In 1937, Ouspensky and his wife left London for New York. They taught there until his health began to fail.

In 1947 he left New York and returned to London. He had been ill for several years and had grown despondent. Perhaps he was affected by the shadow of world events; the Second World War ended with the detonation of two nuclear bombs. As the world emerged from the devastation, tensions were already growing between Russia and the West. The stranglehold of communism was spreading. He had pursued his life's work through two world wars, the communist revolution, and the great depression. He had published numerous books, lectured, taught, and established groups on two continents, but during his last years he was not satisfied. He spoke of not reaching a 'Higher Source'.

During his last two months he spent much of his time in silence. He asked people to take him by car to places in England where he had experienced significant events. He would sit quietly for awhile and then return home.

Ouspensky had been interested in time and recurrence from the beginning. He had written about it in *Tertium Organum*, and again in a novel called *The Strange Life of Ivan Osokin*. In this he wrote of a man who, through the spell of a magician, goes back in time and relives his life with the full knowledge of the consequences of his actions. The knowledge does not prevent him from repeating the same mistakes and poor decisions. The point of the story is that men act with the knowledge of the likely and probable consequences of their actions, but driven by compulsion, desire, and the momentum of previous decisions, they sentence themselves to lives of repeating cycles and reoccurring patterns. Only through a change in one's level of being, resulting from acting in accordance with higher knowledge, could one hope to be free.

During one of his last meetings in London, he said the system as they knew it was incomplete. He gave instructions that they must begin again, and *'return to the source'* that could provide the guidance they needed. Shortly before he died, Ouspensky said to Dr Roles, who was his physician and attended to him during his last days, 'You must go and find a method by which we could achieve Self-realization. If you find the method you may find the source of the Tradition.'[9]

Dr Roles, who was with him during his last moments described how, 'There were prolonged periods of cosmic consciousness before Ouspensky died. During the last two months of his life, Ouspensky received grace for all his work.' He said Ouspensky died in a state of total Self-remembering: 'I saw him reach liberation with my own eyes.' Ouspensky's final hours affected a profound change in Dr Roles, who said Ouspensky had 'done something to him' so that after Ouspensky's death Dr Roles would wake up at night in a different state, and it was then that important realizations came to him that bore the stamp of truth.[10]

Shortly after Ouspensky's passing Dr Roles wrote this poem.

Death
Does fear of death affright the dying
Unprepared to die?
Fears the rope the knot untying?
Death fear not I!
One fear my heart has pain of knowing
Fear of another thing –
That I shall at my hour of going,
Die not remembering.[11]

Ouspensky was remembered by his students as a man of

immense strength and authority. When he spoke to groups his answers were impersonal and succinct. He could be merciless to pretense or artificiality, but he was also a man of humor and charm. If you spoke to him alone of some personal problem, he would always be helpful and benevolent. The owner of a restaurant Ouspensky frequented came to see him when he was ill. He said, 'I can't understand his books, but Mr Ouspensky is the only really kind man I ever met.'[12] The doorman of the building where he lived said he looked forward to seeing him every morning. One student said, 'His will power was immense and his bearing majestic, to be in his presence could be awe-inspiring; to sit on the edge of his silence was like being irradiated by the sunlight of consciousness.' Another student spoke of his presence, 'As being beyond words.'[13] Dr Roles said, 'Ouspensky was the only man I have met that I could trust completely.'[14]

He was a down-to-earth teacher with a phenomenal memory. A student once stood up with notes, saying he had twenty questions. He asked the first question and then waited. Ouspensky waved him on until he had asked all of his questions. Then he answered each question in detail without missing a single question. He was an active man, a good horseman and a crack shot, though he never in his life aimed at a living creature.[15]

During his stay in America he and Madame Sophie Ouspensky lived on a farm in Mendham, New Jersey. Franklin Farms, acquired with the help of several wealthy students was an imposing three story granite house on a hilltop surrounded by 400 acres of farmland. It had been the residence of the former governor of New Jersey. It became the center for Ouspensky's work in the US.

After the death of her husband Madame Ouspensky lived the rest of her life at Franklin Farms. She taught the 'System,' outlined by her husband, and movements and exercises she had learned from Gurdjieff. The publication after his death of his *In Search of the Miraculous*, attracted many.

In speaking about the Work and the movements she taught at Lyne Place in Surrey, England, and Franklin Farms in New Jersey, she said, 'Here we want people with a strong desire. This work requires a special intensity and that needs special conditions. Here we regulate activities, meals, and sleep, to create propitious conditions that those who wish to see may see.' She taught until her death in 1961.[16]

In London, the leadership of The Study Society passed to Dr Francis Roles. Both he and his wife Joan had been educated at Cambridge. He had inherited the efficiency and discipline of his British father and the generous spirit of his American mother.

After the death of her husband Mme. Ouspensky urged Dr Roles and others to return to Gurdjieff, but the doctor was sure that was not Ouspensky's wish. He embraced the knowledge he had been left and would continue 'The Work,' and the search for 'The Source' he had been instructed to find. Some of the students did return to Gurdjieff, others drifted away, but Dr Roles was an inspired leader and soon attracted a group in London of more than three hundred people.

Years later, when Dr Roles sat before a master teacher in India, one of the questions he asked was about Ouspensky. 'Our teacher worked and taught all his life, but although he had searched he said he had not connected with a Higher Source. What happens to such a man?' The teacher, Shantananda Saraswati (see Chapter 13), answered: 'It happens that students pass on before reaching fulfillment and the teacher completes the student's work within himself. In other instances the teacher passes on before completing his work, and his work is completed by a group of devoted followers. You need not worry about the fate of a man who lived the life of Ouspensky.'[17] Years later in response to another question, Shantananda Saraswati said, 'Once a relationship is established between a teacher and a disciple, both will be liberated together. Bodies may seem to leave each other, but in reality the teacher comes again and again until all are liberated simultaneously.'[18]

In 1993 during Shantananda Saraswati's last audience with a member of the Study Society, he concluded by saying, 'My blessings and goodwill for the well-being of this organization, which

MADAME OUSPENSKY
(1878-1961)

If our aim is not formed, we are not in the Work yet. If a man has an aim he makes demands on himself — a man in the Work knows what he wants, knows right from wrong and is determined to achieve his aim — hates sleep and desires to remember himself and takes everything relative to that... You cannot come to consciousness unconsciously. If we see what we have not got we will know what we want — and what effort we must make to get it.

It's Up to Ourselves, Chapter 32.

~23~

was started by a great man who hailed from Russia and who was loved by Dr Roles. When he [Ouspensky] was about to leave his mortal body, he instructed Dr Roles to find a teacher in India. This teaching is ancient, and the tree planted and nourished by him cannot be harmed by any turbulence... Blessings for your welfare.'[19]

During the last year of Ouspensky's life his wife submitted his manuscript, titled *Fragments of an Unknown Teaching*, to Gurdjieff, who warmly approved it and advised her to publish it. It was published in 1949 shortly before Gurdjieff's death.[20] The publisher made the author's title the subtitle and took the title of Ouspensky's lecture series, *In Search of the Miraculous*, as the book title. It reached a wide audience and had a profound affect in Europe and America. It demonstrated the breadth and magnitude of the principles and methods developed by Gurdjieff.

The book expounded a comprehensive view of man and of cosmology, of man's psychology and inner workings. It explained the methods by which men and women with will, perseverance, and the help of a group or school, could work toward liberation from their superficial, petty, and mundane habits to raise the level of awareness and live up to their full potential. The narrative portion of the book describes the interaction of a Middle Eastern teacher and a Russian journalist against the backdrop of the Russian revolution.

Gurdjieff said he would always be grateful to Ouspensky for this book.[21] 'When word of Ouspensky's death reached Gurdjieff, he sat for a long time in silence then said slowly, Ah, Ouspensky! He wrote *Fragments* [*In Search of the Miraculous*] so I love him.'[22] He said Ouspensky had recorded the conversations and the principles he had elucidated with great accuracy.[23] It was all the more impressive as there was no note-taking during meetings with Gurdjieff. Everything had been written from Ouspensky's memory. The book inspired many to seek out groups and begin what has become known as 'The Work'.

Gurdjieff's own writings were published and made available in many languages: *All and Everything*, and *Meetings with Remarkable*

Men are profound, but it was Ouspensky's lucid writings that served to awaken the interest of many. During the fifties and sixties, the writings of Gurdjieff, Ouspensky, as well as their students, Thomas de Hartman, Orage, Maurice Nicoll, Rodney Collin, and others, were published and widely read. They continue to attract men and women to groups on every continent.

WILLEM A. NYLAND
(1890–1975)

The Work begins with a wish, to be more than what I am; because I am dissatisfied with the condition I find myself in, bound by habit, forgetting who and what and even where I am. It is not enough to live in this ordinary state. I wish to wake up! To awaken a faculty, to create an 'I' that can observe myself, in the moment, right now where I Am. An 'I' that is impartial, not bound by judgments or criticism. It is myself that I remember, it is my birthright! But it is only mine when I make an effort. You must make efforts; your life depends upon it.

It is not enough to say I forget. Take some action to remember. Put a pebble in your shoe, put the tool in the other hand for awhile, walk a block out of your way, go against the grain, against the mechanical habits.

You must make efforts!

Mr Nyland did not like to be quoted. The above phrases are not a direct quote but the author's memory of a theme he spoke of often.

4

Willem A. Nyland

Firefly

URDJIEFF INSPIRED many to continue with his work.
In New York, one of them was Willem Nyland. Dutch by
birth, he immigrated to the US between the wars. He met
Gurdjieff in New York in 1924 and remained in contact with him
from then on until Gurdjieff's death in 1949. In 1947, Gurdjieff gave
him material and instructions to establish a group in New York
City, which grew into the Gurdjieff Foundation. Working with Mr
and Mrs Thomas de Hartmann, Mrs Jeane de Salzmann, Dr Welch,
and others, groups were established in New York and other cities.
The Work was shaped into a system of meetings, groups, and
classes in movements. Gurdjieff had gathered these movements
and dances in his travels and they were accompanied by piano
music that had been composed by Gurdjieff in collaboration with
Thomas de Hartman.

Nyland was a Renaissance man. In many ways he reminded me
of Leon MacLaren (see Chapter 7). Both men composed music and
played the piano. Both developed skills in architecture, building,
business, and had the charisma and natural teaching ability to
attract and inspire many students. Nyland purchased a two-room
cottage on six acres in Brewster, NY, and each summer he and his
brother in-law, working with their hands, added to the buildings.

Later, groups of students came to work. Under his guidance, a twenty-room pavilion was completed with a music room and an art studio for his wife. There they raised their children. A chemist by profession, he had earned a doctorate from Columbia University. Some called him Dr Nyland.

He was outspoken and sometimes strident about what he believed were misstatements and misunderstandings on the part of his colleagues and would often devote entire lectures to such issues. He spoke directly and forcefully. For example, when the Work began to be described as a 'new way of thinking', he was dismayed and appeared angered. He explained at great length and with unassailable logic that self-awareness was neither thought, feeling, or sensation, but rather 'a new faculty of being'.

In the sixties, he left the Foundation and in time established groups of his own in New York, Boston, New Mexico, and San Francisco. He purchased thirteen acres of land with a large barn that had a gabled roof in upstate New York. There he built a house on the property and moved from his home in Brewster to take up residence at the 'Chardavogne Barn'. The group called the house 'Firefly'. Students from around the country began to move there to engage in The Work with Nyland. They had families and established businesses. The barn was renovated and became a center for their activities.

Under his guidance, life and The Work in the group was intense and fruitful. There was a pioneer spirit and conditions were special. The group gathered at the barn on Saturdays and Sundays, arriving at about 7:30 am to have coffee and socialize. There was a meeting at 8:00 am, and afterwards the group would divide into teams for the day's activity. There was much construction work. The huge barn was renovated, a large deck built and other buildings were erected on the property to house crafts and businesses. There was little money for lumber and one of the activities left a vivid impression. There were many obsolete barns in the area, and the group undertook the demolition of these buildings in return for a small fee and the salvaged lumber. Over forty men would arrive at a neighbor's barn with trucks and equipment; ropes were tied to the four walls, the main beams were cut with chainsaws and by lunch the building was pulled to the ground. We returned for a meal eaten at long tables on the second floor of the barn. After lunch Nyland would speak and remind us that whatever activity we were engaged in was a secondary purpose of our day. The primary activity was to be present, to connect through the senses to everything around us, to observe the moving body, as well as our thoughts and feelings, and in all, and in everything, 'to remember myself'.

He taught a method of self-observation so that at any given moment one could awaken a faculty to observe oneself and the surrounding circumstances. This witnessing consciousness would operate in the present. The moment of awareness is free of past thoughts, plans for the future, or daydreams. It is observing what is happening now. The observation is impartial – there is no judgment or evaluation. It is a simple observation of what 'is'. This faculty, this witness he called 'I', could be awakened at any moment simply by the desire to do so. As in many other things, this faculty grows stronger with practice. One begins to recognize that this witnessed consciousness, this observer is, in truth, what I am. Under observation, it is apparent that what I usually refer to as 'I' is the role I play – father, student, teacher, employee. These things are all constantly changing. Through observation one begins to realize that what is observed is not what I am. What I am is the consciousness, the witness, the impartial observer. Awakening this observer is what Nyland called 'remembering myself'. He used the analogy of a firefly, which through an act of will created moments of illumination for himself and the area around him. Having this self-cognizance available during one's daily activities increases awareness, enhances life, and quickens the rate of development.

Lunch ended with a toast, 'To Gurdjieff', and a shot of Armagnac, which was Gurdjieff's liquor of choice. We then listened to Nyland play the piano, after which we returned to work. Some of the women participated in the construction labor, though most worked in the gardens, prepared the meal and did administrative work. The men returned to the neighbor's property to sort and load the lumber on trucks. These were exciting days that had a quality similar to the barn raisings of early American communities. At 3:30 pm we would break for coffee and then go to the barn for movement classes.

Gurdjieff collected sacred dances, special exercises, and music that had a powerful affect. We stood in rows with a teacher and piano player up front and learned a series of precise positions and movements executed in time to the piano. Some mental calculations based on the Law of Seven and the Enneagram (see Appendix 2, page 140) were required. The powerful music gathered by Gurdjieff in his travels was arranged for piano in collaboration with Thomas de Hartman. The movements required full participation of the body and mind, while the emotions responded to the music. They could only be done with the finest quality of attention – if the mind wandered for a split second you would be either out of step or in the wrong position. The effect of these classes was to integrate the function of mind, heart, and body, and heighten awareness to a state rarely experienced. These sessions were so extraordinary that for three months I attended a Wednesday evening course that required a six-hour round trip from the city to attend a one-hour class. On Saturdays, after the movement class, people returned to homes in the area and then gathered again at 7:30 pm for a talk by Nyland, followed by his music. The group met two or three times during the week, and also met once a week in small numbers of four to six people to speak about their studies and their Work. The Work generated great excitement and intensity, indeed, a sense of adventure. We knew conditions were exceptional, and the opportunity we were given could be short-lived. It occurred to some of us that what we were experiencing was similar to what had transpired fifty years before at The Institute in France under Gurdjieff's guidance, an institute that had come to an abrupt end when Gurdjieff had a near-fatal auto accident.

5

Forty Days

T HE RAIN never stopped. For three days and nights the heavens cleansed the earth, at times a deluge, at others a drizzle. Dark clouds, lightning, and thunder rolled across the sky driven by gusting winds. He had labored for breath throughout the storm. On the third day just before dawn Willem Nyland died. The rain stopped, and the sun rose in a clear sky. The year was 1975. He was eighty-four and had been ill for several months. Still, his passing was a shock. He had been teaching this group for a dozen years, and he had taught them to the very end. Before the storm began, he struggled, with labored breathing, to record a taped message to the group in which he encouraged them to continue their Work.

During the last years of his life he had reached out to the Gurdjieff Foundation located in New York City. As a result, communication and collaboration had been established. Many of their leaders came to his funeral which took place in the barn, where a tape of an organ piece he had composed was played. He was buried in a simple coffin built by two men with love and tears. A stone near his home in Brewster where he often sat was moved to the cemetery. A brass plate was engraved and set in the stone where it rested at the head of his grave. In a eulogy at his graveside, his good friend Dr William Welch* said: 'When a

*Dr William J. Welch, 1911-1997, was the attending physician at Gurdjieff's death in Paris in 1949. He graduated from Yale and Columbia Medical School. His autobiography is titled➤

man of substance dies, the sympathy goes to those who are left
behind.'

A few months before, Nyland had spoken of his legacy. His
work would continue. He had known Gurdjieff for twenty-five
years. For fifty years he had taught, striven with all his being that
the wisdom of the wisest of mankind would be actualized in the
lives of men and woman who had come to him to learn. For this
group the baton had passed from Gurdjieff to Nyland until he
passed on.

After his death the group gathered each morning at the center
where he had lived and taught, and where they had worked,
studied, and striven to become more than they had been. They had
relocated from around the country to this small town in upstate
New York to learn from Nyland. They had come, established
homes, businesses, families.

People moved quietly about the barn and property. Speaking in
subdued voices, mourning in small groups or alone; contemplating what they had been given. He left them a legacy: an institute
that he founded with land and buildings, a large barn with a
gabled roof had been renovated and served as a center for their
activities. He left them the Work, the music, and the movements
and he had established groups around the country. His meetings
had been recorded: over two-thousand six hundred tapes of
ninety-minute talks, many transcribed and indexed according to
subject. The lending library in the barn sent tapes and transcripts
to individuals and groups around the continent. He left men and
women who would continue the Work; to teach, to learn and to
live according to what he had taught them.

Each morning they gathered at the barn to mourn, to remember, and to continue the Work. On the first morning a few were

What Happened In Between: A Doctor's Story. In 1984 he succeeded Lord John Pentland as
leader of the Gurdjieff Foundation in New York and served until his death in 1997. In a
eulogy he was described as a man who considered it an astonishing privilege to live, to
think carefully about things, and to be in touch with others. He never took his life or his
companions for granted; for him living was an unspeakable joy.

inspired to read his words aloud. A resolve emerged from them to sound his words twenty-four hours a day for forty days. So a schedule was posted, people filled in their times, and in a small room next to the library, throughout the day and night, his words were spoken and heard. *He had told them that for forty days after death there was a bond between the deceased and loved ones.* The connection was felt throughout the group. They gathered daily at the barn and carried on as they had before. Many remarkable things happened during that time, and I would like to share one of them with you.

One Saturday afternoon a group of some seventy people had finished lunch. Nyland had often spoken to us after lunch and so a tape of one of his short talks was played. It ended, as he had always done, with a toast 'To Gurdjieff', and we each tossed back a shot of Armagnac. I stepped out onto the deck outside the barn overlooking the property; a deck I had spent several weekends helping to build. A car arrived. A man got out and stood awhile leaning against the car staring at the building. He'd driven two hours and now was undecided if he wanted to enter the building; a place he had not been in for several years. I remembered the last large meeting he attended with Nyland, where he asked a question to which Nyland responded to him directly and force-fully. He said Bob was sitting on the fence; one could not learn carpentry by merely being in the company of carpenters; one needed to pick up the tools and work in earnest. He urged him to make greater efforts. The direction had not been gentle; the intent had been to push him off the fence. Bob did not attend another meeting.

Yet here he was in the parking lot, undecided, 'sitting on the fence'. For over a year Bob and I had met in the city with a few others for an hour one morning a week before going to work; we exchanged observations about our studies and our Work. I wanted to help, so I went out and greeted him. We spoke for awhile, and I told him about the conversations being read and invited him to join us for a few minutes.

We walked through the barn and entered the small room where five people were sitting around a table with a pile of manuscripts. They nodded as we sat down. A lady finished reading an answer and paused, then began reading the next question and answer. Bob and I looked at each other in recognition. She was reading Bob's question and Nyland's answer from the last meeting Bob had attended. Bob listened intently as Nyland responded directly to him again. When she finished reading the answer, she paused and then passed the manuscript to another lady, who began to read the next question. I followed as Bob got up to leave. Some in the group realized what had happened. The reader said to me, 'That was his question?' 'Yes,' I answered. She smiled, a few in the room shrugged. There had been many extraordinary events during the forty days. As we walked back to the car I said, 'Twenty-six hundred meetings!'

'That was no coincidence', Bob said. 'I thought about borrowing that tape from the library and listening to his answer, but I decided I didn't want to hear it again. Perhaps I didn't hear it the first time.' I smiled, 'Apparently Mr Nyland wanted you to hear it again.' We shook hands, he got in his car and I watched him drive away. Like an outside observer, I watched my body walk back to the barn. I remembered myself, and I remembered Mr Nyland. He was a remarkable man.

ANDREW MACLAREN
(1883-1975)

Wealth results from work. There is no such thing as a 'windfall'. When one acquires wealth without work or great wealth with little work, others are being deprived of the fruits of their labor. A community without justice will not survive: to each must be rendered his due. A society, through its laws and institutions, must inhibit one man from harvesting the crop of another, that each may reap what he has sown.

Author's memory of a lecture given in by John Allen, quoting Andrew MacLaren, New York, 1992.
Portrait by Jeffrey Courtney.

6

Andrew MacLaren

Standing for Justice

I N LONDON, during the Great Depression, another group was awakening. It began with a member of parliament, Andrew MacLaren. Born in 1883 in an impoverished section of Glasgow, Scotland, the dire conditions he witnessed shaped his viewpoint. After World War I, the masses suffered under an economic depression that lasted nearly twenty years. MacLaren sought to address what he saw as great injustice.

He became a champion of reform, following the economic principles of Henry George, author of *Progress and Poverty* and other writings, which had been influential in America, Europe, China, and Australia. At the height of his popularity, Henry George ran for Mayor of New York City and received a third of the vote. His ideas were opposed by the wealthiest members of society and their political allies.

George followed the classical economists like Adam Smith in recognizing that wealth was the product of work on land and natural resources, with the aid of capital. But he also realized why economic development caused wealth and poverty to increase side by side. Further, he saw that this maldistribution of wealth could be resolved through a change in the tax laws, with the added advantage of ensuring that sites were put to their most productive use by discouraging land speculation that led to periodic booms and busts. He argued that the increase in land value arising from the cumulative work of the community should benefit the community as a whole, and not just those who owned the land. In all areas of commerce he sought to ensure justice by using the law to promote competition and to curtail monopoly and restraint of trade.

Alaska provides a contemporary example of the benefits that would follow. The state constitution vests ownership of all mineral rights in the citizens jointly. Thus the rights to undiscovered oil and other minerals that have been in the earth for millions of years do not become the property of the landowner (as in other parts of the United States). When a mineral resource is discovered, a renewable license to develop it is sold by the state government to the highest bidder. Speculators who attempt to control supply, regulate price, or diminish competition risk losing their license. With the huge profits from oil and other mineral resources, there are many bidders for these licenses. The tax (licensing fee) provides much of the income needed by state and local government, so that there is no need for a state income tax or sales tax and every citizen gets an annual dividend check that represents a share of the profits from oil, gas, and other minerals.

This system has worked for all interests and allowed for an efficient development of the resources and an equitable sharing of the wealth. During the Reagan administration there was an attempt to apply these principles to the harvesting of lumber and other mineral resources on federally owned land. But the measures that were passed met the opposition of wealthy special interest groups and were repealed. Reagan also changed the tax laws to eliminate some of the tax breaks that promote land speculation. These changes were once again opposed by powerful lobbies and repealed. Georgist economic principles have been introduced in diluted form into some of the 'rust belt' cities in Pennsylvania, including Pittsburg, with beneficial results.

Hong Kong's outstanding economic growth owed much to

the high level of government revenue received from land rents (as envisaged by George). Typically the owner of a commercial site holds a lease that grants him exclusive use of the property for a fixed period (ten years or more). At the end of the period the 'owner' has the right to renew the lease. However, if developments in the intervening years have increased the value of the site, the new rent will reflect this increase (In the US and Europe the private land owner reaps the benefit by increasing the rent he charges his tenants). Thus in Hong Kong rising land values and higher rentals, resulting from government expenditures on infrastructure and the cumulative work of the community, increase government revenue rather than enriching private landowners and property speculators. In this way, instead of handing owners of commercial sites an unearned increment, many of functions of government can be funded without burdening the people and the economy with excessive and repressive taxes.

The building of Hong Kong's new, larger airport affords an example of how this works in practice. The old one built on the edge of the city had become inadequate as the city expanded to surround it. To make this possible, as leases expired on the land needed, the city government re-allocated that land for the new airport. They were able to undertake the massive infrastructure project, including new highway and a mass transit system, confident that they could afford it because they knew that the improvements would increase rental values in the surrounding areas, thus affording the government extra revenue to pay for the work.

Under existing tax systems in most other countries, governments do not recoup the cost of infrastructure developments in this way. Instead the increased land values accrue as a windfall to private land owners, leaving the taxpayer to service the high borrowing costs. Hong Kong had a further advantage; the land vacated by the old airport was divided into valuable commercial or residential sites and leased.

Andrew MacLaren

Andrew MacLaren was elected to Parliament as a member of the Independent Labour Party in 1922, resigning from the party in 1943. He remained a member of parliament until 1945. Even as a member of the Labour Party, he was firmly against the welfare state. He believed it was not the role of government to redistribute wealth but to ensure a level playing field so that no individual or company gained an unfair advantage. 'I have emphasized the equal rights of all and mercilessly attacked state doles... I have stood for the untaxing of industry and houses. The taxation of land I have persistently advocated.'

> The home is the place where a woman has to bring forth her children and the place in which little children touch the knee and ask the first question and receive the first answer. It is the home that marks the beginning of spiritual development of the race. How is it that the tabernacle of the family should be burdened with taxes?[1]

He believed social engineering and central planning appeared necessary due to the prevailing inequities of the economic system. As he saw it, without reforming the land-tenure system, the welfare state would bankrupt the government (the debt burdening many European nations today suggests he may have been right). He sought to make the land and its natural resources less a pleasure ground for the rich and more a treasure trove for the nation. He was a strong supporter of the introduction of land value taxation in the 1931 Finance Act. As in the US, the measure was opposed by powerful interests and repealed a few years later. In 1937 he tried to introduce a land value taxation bill but was narrowly defeated. Andrew MacLaren's biography, *Standing for Justice*, by John Stewart, reveals a man with an innate sense of justice, who devoted his life to understanding the causes of poverty and promoting the measures needed to eradicate it. He regarded freedom of fundamental importance, both for the individual and for society. He drew no distinction between civil freedom, economic freedom, and freedom of religion. He believed these freedoms were inherent in man's nature, and that the role of government, through laws and institutions, was to ensure and protect these freedoms, often compromised by ignorance and greed.

He supported the founding, by his son Leon, of the School of Economic Science in London, with the object of promoting 'the study of the natural laws governing the relations between men in society'. The purpose was to restore justice to a failing economic system that had broken down in America and Europe. Unemployment was over twenty percent, with shortages of food and many other commodities. The financial system had collapsed, resulting in the loss of people's savings, and a lack of credit that had ground the economy to a halt. Prices were decreasing annually by as much as ten percent, and market prices for produce were too low for farmers to subsist. In America, farmers were burning crops and refusing to send produce to market in a desperate attempt to raise prices while people in the city stood in soup lines to avoid starvation. Many were considering replacing capitalism with either fascism or communism. In 1932, on the day President Roosevelt was inaugurated, the *New York Times* wrote a front page editorial urging him to declare an emergency and assume dictatorial powers.

My father told the story of a woman who once a week asked a butcher for bones and scraps to feed her dog. The butcher knew there was no dog, but he gave her packages with generous portions of meat left on the bone. She added potatoes and vegetables and cooked a stew for her family that staved off hunger for a few days each week. MacLaren's son, Leon, once described the hardships being suffered in London, 'It was the sort of grueling poverty where a mother could buy either food or soap for she did not have enough for both'. It was in this economic climate that the School of Economic Science was founded. Students sought an understanding of the natural laws of economics with the aim of showing how the problems of poverty and injustice might be resolved peacefully. The School was governed by the highest of moral principles. No one drew a salary or received any economic gain. It attracted men and women who studied and worked selflessly and anonymously to uplift society.*

---

* The author would like to acknowledge the work of Neil Broxmeyer, a leader of the School of Practical Philosophy in New York, and John Allen, a senior student and tutor at the School of Economic Science in London. They spent years teaching economic study groups the principles expounded by Henry George, Andrew and Leon MacLaren, and the writings of the classical economists, Adam Smith , David Ricardo and others. Their work allowed students to gain clarity and understanding of the economic principles that govern so much of our daily life.

LEON MACLAREN
(1910-1994)

Everything begins in the Absolute which holds all possibilities within itself. When the consciousness of man loses connection with the Source, then there are difficulties. The same applies to nations. The forces that bind a society are law, language, and religion. These are held in the consciousness of the people. As mankind loses its connection with his true nature, the forces that bind a society are weakened. One begins to see the relationship between the spiritual state of mankind and the condition of the family, the community, and the nation.

Author's memory of a talk given in Wallkill, New York, 1988.
Photograph used with the kind permission of Vececslav Stanuga.

7

Leon MacLaren

A School is Born

LEON MACLAREN was inspired by his father's idealism. The love of justice and truth was the passion of his life. He wanted to work to help humanity. At the age of sixteen, in a moment of contemplation, he questioned how his life could best be put to the service of mankind. A one-word answer was revealed, the word was 'School'. Years later, in 1936, aided by his father's reputation and with his help, he began an economic study group based on the Socratic method of inquiry that became The School of Economic Science. He was a man with a commanding presence, a barrister by profession, a gifted speaker, and an inspired teacher. His charisma attracted a circle of devoted students.

When he realized that the study of economics did not answer many of the questions he and his students were asking, he expanded the school's course of study. He concluded that in order to establish justice and lift a nation there must be knowledge of man's essential nature. For this he turned to philosophy and began a study of Plato, Shakespeare, and Scripture.

His quest for justice and truth overshadowed a promising career in law and politics. He worked only six weeks a year as a barrister to support himself and devoted the rest of his time to directing the School in London and guiding the work of students who were establishing schools in other countries. His father had hoped his brilliant son would pursue a legal and political career, seeing in him the strength and talent to lead a nation. Commenting on his son's chosen path, he remarked: 'Some men lose their sons to drink; my son pursued philosophy.'[1]

In 1953, six years after Ouspensky's death, Leon MacLaren was introduced by his wife to Dr Roles, who now led the Study Society. MacLaren recognized the value of the knowledge that had been acquired from Gurdjieff and Ouspensky and the Work that had gone on in The Study Society. Over the next few years he was taught the 'System' by Dr Roles, and the two groups worked together in close cooperation.

MacLaren proved to be a master teacher and an inspired leader. He had a facility for expressing the esoteric concepts of Gurdjieff and Ouspensky in a way that made them accessible to people who had had no previous contact with either of these men or their writings. Using many of their concepts and diagrams, MacLaren organized the material as a course in philosophy extending over a number of terms. In this way, the Law of Seven, the Law of Three, the Three Centers of Man, levels of consciousness and other concepts that were the essence of the 'System' were unfolded in stages. Each session included practical exercises designed to raise the level of awareness that gave many students the experience of remembering themselves.

This material was powerful and effective. The philosophy classes became more popular than the economics classes, and the School began to grow. Schools of Philosophy also sprang up in other countries, where this material remained virtually unchanged for thirty years, introducing many people to 'The Work'.[2]

The philosophy material never quoted or acknowledged Gurdjieff, Ouspensky, Dr Roles, or Leon MacLaren. This reflected an understanding held by all four that the truth could not be personalized: it belonged to no one man, it belonged to all mankind.

Although Leon MacLaren never met Gurdjieff or Ouspensky, through Dr Roles he acquired a profound understanding and respect for what they taught. Towards the end of his life he reread all of Ouspensky's works and had a keen interest in *The Strange Life of Ivan Osokin.*[3]

However, from the early 1960s, the School came under the guidance of a new teacher. Ever since the death of Ouspensky, Dr Roles had followed his instruction to 'search for the source'. Several teachers came to London, but they were not the source for which Dr Roles was searching. Soon, however, he was led to India. That part of Leon MacLaren's story is told in Chapter 15.

ADI SHANKARA
(788 AD-820 AD)

There is One Omnipotent Eternal Consciousness.
Brahman, The Absolute, is Consciousness.
Atman, The Self, is Consciousness.
Consciousness is that which creates All.
Consciousness is that which sustains All.
When Consciousness is withdrawn from anything
in the creation, that form ceases to exist.

Drawn from *Brahma Sutras Bhasya* of Shankara.

8

Adi Shankara

ADI SANKARA, born about twelve hundred years ago in India, was a philosopher, a mystic, a founder of monastic orders, a national hero, and an Avatar. Above all he is recognized as a master teacher who was able to indicate the way to liberation from illusion, bondage, and recurrence, and to the realization of the highest aim of human existence. He revived and codified the tradition of *Advaita Vedanta* in India. He wrote commentaries on the *Upanishads*, the *Brahma Sutras* and the *Bhagavad Gita*, as well as his own philosophical treatises.

Adi Shankara traveled throughout India teaching and engaging in debate the learned masters of many philosophical traditions. Through his writings, teaching, and debates, he restored a respect for the philosophy of non-dualism, and ushered in a new era in the history of India.

He was born to an aged, childless couple, who led a devout life of service to the poor, and had prayed for a child. They named the child Shankara, which means 'giver of prosperity'. Those who visited the newborn were in awe of his divinity, and throughout his childhood all agreed that this was no ordinary child. At the age of five he entered the religious tradition of Brahmacharya.

During his short life of thirty-three years, he traveled the length and breadth of India teaching the philosophy of *Advaita** (non-dualism) wherever he went.

* *Advaita* literally means 'not two'.

He said:

Just as fire is the direct cause of cooking, so without knowledge no emancipation can be had. Compared with all other disciplines, knowledge of the Self is the most direct means of liberation. Let the man of understanding strive for liberation, abandoning desire for the enjoyment of external aims and pleasures. When the force of desire for the Truth blossoms, selfish desires wither away, just like darkness vanishes before the radiance of the light of dawn.

One should become aware of oneself, indivisible, and perfect; free from identification with all things transient, such as one's body, functions, mind, and the sense of being the doer, for all these are the product of ignorance.[1]

To preserve the tradition, he established seats of wisdom in four of the cultural centers of India, one in the north, south, east, and west. To each he appointed one of his principal disciples, who became known as a Shankaracharya (a teacher in the tradition of Shankara). Each master teacher prepared a successor, and a lineage was established that continues to the present day.

According to legend Shankara asked his teacher, 'What are your final words for me? What exactly is the mission you want me to accomplish?'

Govinda, his teacher, replied:

Be fearless, let fearlessness radiate from you and dispel fear in the hearts of others.

Do not be a threat to others or consider others to be a threat to you. Deliver only the message of the sages that you have received directly or what has been revealed in the Vedas and the Upanishads.

Neither force nor manipulate others into following you. Rather dedicate your life to the highest truth and let the magnetism of truth itself pull people to you.

Do not teach principles that you do not practice. Resolve any contradiction between your direct experience and the words of the wise. Only then may you teach those principles.

It is not important to teach all that you know, teach what people need to know, and what they are ready to receive. Guide them so they improve their lives, become stronger, increase their capacities, gain deeper insight, and progressively become worthy to receive and appreciate higher wisdom. Be a constant traveler. Wherever you go, find out what people are missing and how it can be provided. In all things remember harmlessness.

From now on this earth is your bed, your arms are your pillows, the sky is the roof under which you sleep, the sun and the moon are your lamps, and dispassion is your life's companion. Without being burdened by worldly possessions, be the emperor of the universe.

May eternal peace be yours![2]

SHRI GURUDEVA –
SWAMI BRAHMANANDA SARASWATI
(1870-1953)

I have always traveled the straight path of renunciation. When God gives, He gives all that is required. The one who has come, has to go. Nobody can stay here. Every moment keep your luggage packed, nobody knows when death will call. One should always be cautious so that one has no regrets at the time of death. When the mind realizes God, it is permanently established there and one does not desire other things.

Online Quotes, Swami Brahmanada Saraswati.

9

Shri Gurudeva –
Swami Brahmananda
Saraswati

URING THE nineteenth and the first half of the twentieth
century, the seat of wisdom in the Jyotirmath monastery
in Northern India had remained empty because no one
suitable had been found to fill the role. To remedy the situation, in
1940 the religious leaders of India instituted a search for an enlight-
ened Master who could occupy the seat. According to tradition it
could only be filled by:

One who was born in a renowned Brahmin family.
One linked by the Guru-disciple lineage to a Shankaracharya
Math.
One who had entered an ascetic order.
A master of the Vedic scriptures, upright, intelligent, intellectual,
and was able to uphold the principle of Advaita or Cosmic
Oneness.
One free of desire, fully self-controlled, and an expert in the
techniques of yoga or union with the Divine.[1]

Their search finally led to Shri Gurudeva, who was born on
December 21, 1870, on the winter solstice – the longest night of the

year. On that day the earth reaches the maximum northward tilt on its axis. Each day thereafter the earth moves back on its axis and the days grow longer. In some traditions the day is celebrated as a returning of the light. On the solstice, if you draw a line through the equator it points to the center of our galaxy. Some say on this day the earth resembles a head bowed in devotion to the heart of the galaxy. It is regarded as a most propitious day for a soul to be born.

He was a child saint. At the age of nine he left his Brahmin family in search of God. A policeman seeing a boy traveling alone returned him to his home. He asked his parents to allow him to leave home and pursue a spiritual life. His parents took him to a respected teacher in the hopes that he would be dissuaded. The boy exhibited wisdom far beyond his years, an inner light and power radiated from him. The teacher advised the parents to allow him to follow his path. Two days later he left his home and set out in search of a teacher. Five years later, after meeting several teachers, he walked to the Himalayas where he met Swami Krishnanada Saraswati and soon became his favorite disciple. Under his master's guidance he retired to live in a cave with a resolve not to return to the *ashram* until he had reached enlightenment. He lived in the cave for nine years before emerging.

With the passing of years his wisdom and power matured and people came to him for guidance. At the age of seventy, a group of learned Brahmins sought him out and implored him to fill the chair that had been empty for 165 years. Having no desire for position or ceremonial function, he withdrew again to a hermitage. He was approached again and entreated to make his wisdom available to mankind. He is reported to have said, 'You want to put in chains a lion who has moved about the forest freely. But I honor your words, and am ready to assume the responsibility and serve the cause for which Adi Shankara stood.'[2] He fully dedicated himself to this mission and as Shankaracharya of the North, (one of the four seats of wisdom established by Adi Shankara) he was revered throughout India.

Gurudeva said:

A human body is attained with great difficulties. Being born in human species is the only way out of the prison of birth and death. If one misses this opportunity out of negligence, lethargy, and hesitation, one is bound to undergo the plight of birth and death again. Hence arise, awake, attain eternal peace and bliss by being in contact with the best of mankind.[3]

In 1945, at the end of the Second World War, he was interviewed by a journalist who asked him his view on the great victory over tyranny. Gurudeva's response is worth quoting in full.

Real victory is that, after which, there can never be a reverse. Nobody can call himself a victor forever by merely crushing an external foe, because such foes can spring up again. A real victory is achieved by bringing under control the internal foes. A check over the internal enemies is therefore the only way of conquering the external enemies forever, because we should bear in mind that it is our internal enemies that create the external enemies. These internal enemies are ambition, anger, greed, false attachment, vanity, and jealousy. It is this hexagon sitting inside us which makes a cat's paw of anything in the outer world in order to create enemies for us. Therefore if anyone wants to enjoy peace and happiness through victory over all external enemies he should raid the very source of all physical enemies – the subtle hexagon living in us. Destruction of enemies by root is not possible without breaking up this hexagon. This is axiomatic. For a nation which desires to be free from enemies and to build a world of peace and happiness, it is necessary to have leaders who have conquered their inner hexagon. Otherwise they would destroy themselves along with many others. The history of the last several centuries has shown that leaders of powerful nations have given a blood bath to the world under the influence of their hexagon. This is brutish. Those who carry the burden of guiding a nation should particularly act with insight. It is no greatness or humanism to be carried away by one's hexagon and spread a wave of suffering over the earth.

For the liquidation of this subtle cell of inner enemies, which provides a breeding place to all the external enemies, it is not necessary to start a slaughter which keeps the world hanging between life and death. The only thing necessary is to be unbiased and act guided by reason. A person is unbiased who looks correctly, and sees things as they are. There is no difference between what a thing is and how he sees it. His outlook is completely balanced. His appreciation of a thing is correct – in other words, he never misunderstands.

He discriminates between what is eternal and what is transitory. By saying the world is unreal, we mean that it can exist as it is only for the time being, and that it would look something different hereafter. Everybody is actually seeing that everything in the world perishes and that we shall have to miss it one day – the smallest and the biggest are all destined to change.

One who has set in his heart the concept of the transitory nature of the world through a process of reasoning and deep thought, is the person competent to win over the inner hexagon. Because one who is convinced that the entire world is transitory cannot be susceptible to greed or attachment to anything, for he knows that the object of his greed or attachment today will be something different tomorrow. It is this inner victory for which man should strive.[4]

How relevant his warning was! Over the next four decades the contest between the super powers demonstrated the danger of power without knowledge, and knowledge without virtue.

Several sages of the generation before Gurudeva had said that, with the beginning of a new Yuga (cycle), the time was propitious for the East to reach out to the West. Having lived through two World Wars and the detonation of two nuclear bombs that destroyed Hiroshima and Nagasaki, between 1945 and 1947 Gurudeva developed a modified practice of meditation, suitable to the householder engaged in the affairs of everyday life.[5]

The traditional practice of meditation prior to this was part of a set of arduous disciplines practiced by ascetics. It involved long periods of solitude and inner contemplation and was practiced in seclusion or in a monastic setting. The student spent years practicing physical exercises, hatha yoga, that prepared him to sit cross-legged, erect, and still, for hours. This practice was not practical for most people in the East or the West.

Gurudeva taught this modified form of meditation to his disciples. Among them were Shantananda Saraswati and Maharishi Mahesh Yogi. During the last moments of his life he told Maharishi, 'What I have taught you also contains the knowledge of the technique [the meditation] for the householder.'[6] After Gurudeva's death in 1953, following directions left in his will, Shantananda Saraswati succeeded him as the Shankaracharya of the North. Maharishi Mahesh Yogi, who became widely known as 'The Maharishi', was inspired by his teacher to take on a special task. In 1959 he traveled to Europe to introduce Transcendental Meditation to the West. His endeavor to promulgate the practice of meditation proved remarkably successful.

SWAMI SATCHIDANANDA
(1914-2002)

The East has met the West.

Woodstock music festival, 1969.
Photo published with permission Integral Yoga Multimedia.

10

Vedanta and
Western Philosophy*

HE PHILOSOPHY of India had influenced eminent minds in
the West long before Gurudeva. The invasion of India by
Alexander the Great in 310 BC brought with it the influence
of Indian philosophy to the Greeks. Alexander studied with Indian
teachers and brought one sage back with him to Babylon. He once
wrote to an Indian king, 'The Brahmins are the only good men.'
There were Indian slaves in Athens and a large number of Indian
troops in the Persian army that invaded Greece in 480 BC. A letter
of one of Plato's students speaks of conversations between
Socrates and a Brahmin. To students of the Upanishads, it is evident that Pythagoras, Parmenides, and Plato, were familiar with
the universal principles expressed in Vedanta.[1]

* This chapter grew out of a conversation with Cedric Grigg. He and his wife Evelyn
founded and led the School of Philosophy in Boston. They raised four children, whom he
supported by working for a pharmaceutical company. Many of their students felt they were
a part of their extended family. Later they founded a school in Rochester, New York. They
have devoted their lives to teaching this Work and have been a source of inspiration to
many. A detailed account of the influence of the Vedanta Philosophy on Western philosophers is the subject of *The Journey of the Upanishads to the West* by Swami Tathagatananda.
During the twentieth century many teachers came to America and raised awareness of the
philosophy of Vedanta. Among them were Krishnamurti, Sai Baba, Shri Chimnoy,
Bhaktivedanta – Srila Prabupada (who introduced Hare Krishna chant) and Swami Rama
(founder of The Himilayan Institute). Their stories are told in *American Veda* by Philipe
Goldberg.

An English translation of the *Bhagavad Gita* was published in London in 1785; translations into Latin, German, and French followed. They were read by scholars in Europe and America. During the Enlightenment Movement in America, John Adams' letters to Thomas Jefferson recorded his deep interest in Indian Philosophy. Emerson, Thoreau and Walt Whitman drew inspiration from the *Bhagavad Gita*.

Emerson, who would one day be called the sage of Concord, read widely of the history, beliefs and religious practices of India. Of the *Bhagavad Gita* he wrote in his journal in 1831, 'It was the first of books; it was as if an empire spoke to us, the voice of an old intelligence that in another age pondered the same questions that exercise us.' From his studies he extracted the idea that the Universe is an emanation of divine power and that the purpose of human life is for the soul to realize its essential unity with its source. In his writings and lectures Emerson gave expression to Vedantic principles.[2]

> In his later writings it is practically impossible to separate the Eastern and Western components; Indian monism and Western idealism, the Hindu Atman and the Western Self, Oriental mysticism and Neo-Platonism transmuted into Emersonian transcendentalism.

Gandhi was influenced by Emerson whom he read while he was incarcerated in India. Martin Luther King adopted Gandhi's tactic of passive resistance which was based on the Vedantic principle of *ahimsa* (harmlessness).

William James considered Vedantic philosophy 'the paragon of all monastic systems' and quoted Swami Vivekananda, whom he called the paragon of Vedantist missionaries. Vivekananda's presence at the Parliament of World Religions in Chicago in 1893 inspired Western philosophers and religious leaders. Vivekananda toured the Eastern US for two years introducing Yoga (Unity), and the philosophy of Vedanta to America. He established The Vedanta Society in New York City.[3] A brownstone was purchased on West

80th Street in Manhattan which became a center for meditation and the study of Vedanta philosophy. Although that building was sold the Vedanta Society has continued in New York and is active today in countries around the world.

Walt Whitman expressed this same philosophy in his poem titled, 'Song of Myself'.

> Divine am I inside and out, and I make holy
> Whatever I touch or am touched from.
> I am the mate and companion of people,
> All just as immortal and fathomless as myself.

In 1920 Swami Yogananda Paramahansa arrived in America following an invitation to speak in Boston. His speech was titled 'The Science of Religion', and it set the theme for three decades of work during which he established the Self Realization Fellowship, introduced Vedanta to hundreds of thousands of people, and in 1946 published *The Autobiography of a Yogi,* a book that sold over four million copies and lived up to the slogan, 'The book that changed the lives of millions'. SRF continues to flourish after his death in 1952 and now has over five hundred centers in fifty countries that introduce students to the philosophy of Vedanta.

In 1966, Swami Satchidananda, arrived in the US from India. During the next thirty-six years he built an organization that popularized Hatha Yoga. He established Integral Yoga centers in the US that introduced many to Yoga and an Indian philosophy based on the principles of harmony, health, self-discipline, and stillness. He was a charismatic guru who was photographed with popes, priests, ministers, and three US presidents. In 1969, at the three-day Woodstock Music Festival, he appeared on stage to open the event. The bearded guru with a radiant smile gave a blessing, a short talk, and then led 500,000 people through yogic breathing exercises, a Sanskrit chant, and a brief period of meditation. A few hours later, Ravi Shankar enthralled the huge audience playing classical Indian ragas on the sitar. Ten years earlier such events could not have been imagined.

Addressing the gathering of over half a million people, Satchidananda said:

> My beloved sisters and brothers, I am overwhelmed with joy to see the youth of America gathered here... Let us not fight for peace, but let us find peace within ourselves first... Let our activities and all our arts express Yoga [Unity]... If these pictures were shown in India they would not believe they were taken in America, for here the East has met the West.[4]

Indian philosophy had also found an audience among scholars in Germany, France, and Russia. Immanuel Kant, 1712-1804, was a serious student of Hindu philosophy and Sanskrit. Goethe, Schopenhauer, Herman Hesse, and Tolstoy, were all influenced by Indian philosophy.

The educated classes of Europe and America read these writers and were indirectly influenced by the philosophy of the East. *However, the essence of Eastern Spiritual Science is more than inspirational. It is a system, a method, a way of life through which a dedicated student can participate in a process of inner transformation. It is a transcendental journey from limitation to liberation.* Laws and universal principles are revealed, but the Way is more than a theoretical exposition. There are stages of development and clearly prescribed practices and disciplines for each step.

The inspiration of philosophers, writers, and poets helped to stimulate interest, but for the wisdom of the East to take root and grow in the minds and hearts of the West, teachers were needed who had imbibed the esoteric teaching from the ancient lineage of Masters, guardians of this sacred knowledge. Gurdjieff, Ouspensky, Willem Nyland, Dr Roles, and Leon MacLaren were among those in the West who sought out these teachers, acquired knowledge, applied what they learned, and devoted their lives to teaching Eastern esoteric knowledge to the West.

MAHARISHI MAHESH YOGI
(1917-2008)

Happiness radiates like the fragrance of a flower, and
draws all good things towards you.
Allow your love to nourish yourself as well as others.
Do not strain after the needs of life, it is sufficient to be
quietly alert and aware of them.
In this way, life proceeds more naturally and effortlessly.
Life is here to enjoy!

Quote from thinkexist.com.
Photo copyright 2001, Maharishi Foundation.

11
Maharishi Mahesh Yogi
Flower Power – The Spirit of the Sixties

T
HE SIXTIES was a decade of turbulence, social change, and inner exploration. Astrologers spoke of an alignment of planets that heralded the 'Dawning of the Age of Aquarius' – a time of radical change. In 1960 John F. Kennedy was elected as the youngest president in the history of the US. He stepped onto the world stage with a beautiful and regal young wife and two pre-school children. In his inauguration speech he said:

> We stand today on the edge of a New Frontier – the frontier of the 1960s – a frontier of unknown opportunities and peril – a frontier of unfulfilled hopes and threats. Ask not what your country can do for you, but what you can do for your country.

Later, he announced the US would land a man on the moon before the end of the decade. The air was filled with confidence and optimism, but the exuberance was soon overshadowed by the threat of nuclear war and civil unrest.

The nuclear arms race between the US and Russia began at the end of World War II in 1945. During the decades that followed the two nations built tens of thousands of hydrogen bombs. The hydrogen bomb is one thousand times more powerful than the atomic bomb that destroyed Hiroshima. The bombs were mounted on missiles, carried on battle ships, submarines, and planes, and were aimed at cities on every continent. The danger of a nuclear holocaust seemed imminent; at times it appeared inevitable. There was a great sense of urgency. Reasonable men agreed that it was imperative that the super powers step back from the abyss, but there was no certainty they would be able to do so. Addressing the nuclear arms race at the height of the cold war Pope John Paul II, on a visit to Hiroshima said, 'It is only through a conscious and a deliberate policy that humanity can be saved.'[1]

During the fifties and sixties the super powers made plans for nuclear war. The governments built fallout shelters in cities, and a highly publicized campaign encouraged people to build shelters in their homes. In New York, Governor Rockefeller gave tax credits to people who built concrete shelters in their basements; they were stocked with water and provisions so people could wait out the nuclear fallout. As a boy I remember my father looking at plans and considering building a concrete bunker in our basement. In school there were 'drills' where we prepared for a nuclear attack by crawling under our desks and covering our head with our arms. Three popular movies, *Fail Safe*, *On the Beach* and *Dr Strangelove*, depicted the threat of life on the planet being extinguished by nuclear war.

The planet came closest to a nuclear holocaust during the Cuban Missile Crisis. In October of 1962 the world held its breath for thirteen days. The US had installed nuclear missiles in European countries, including in Turkey on the Russian border. In October of 1962, the US took aerial photographs of the Russians installing missiles in Cuba, ninety miles from the US. Adlai Stevenson, the US ambassador to the UN, confronted the Russians with the photographs at the UN General Assembly. The US set up a naval blockade to stop Russian ships from reaching Cuba. Russian and American warships, some armed with nuclear weapons, were set on a collision course. Both militaries took preliminary steps to launch their nuclear missiles. While President Kennedy and Khrushchev tried to avoid what for years had appeared inevitable, some political leaders in both capitals were quietly moving their families to safer locations out of the cities. In the US, 250,000 troops were moved to southern Florida in preparation for an invasion of Cuba. The Cubans were prepared for an invasion. The Americans were unaware that 100,000 Cuban troops were being led by 42,000 Russian troops that had been deployed to Cuba armed with over a hundred nuclear weapons that could be launched from the battlefield.

In the US nuclear defenses were raised to Def Con II, which meant missiles were armed and in launch position and bombers with hydrogen bombs were in the air. At sea an American destroyer detected a Russian submarine near Cuba and attacked with depth charges. The submarine commander believing the war had begun ordered the launch of a nuclear missile. The order was aborted by an on-board political officer during the last minute of the countdown. The counter order averted a nuclear war. President Kennedy and Khrushchev were under pressure from their military leaders to launch the first strike. Kennedy arranged a back door meeting between his brother Robert and a Russian diplomat with personal ties to Khrushchev. They reached an agreement, conceived by Adlai Stevenson, involving secret concessions. In return for the Russians removing the missiles and nuclear weapons from Cuba, the US agreed not to invade Cuba and to quietly remove nuclear missiles from Turkey six months later. This last minute agreement ended a crisis that could have killed much of the world's population.

The assassination of President Kennedy in 1963 was followed by the murder of Martin Luther King and Robert Kennedy in 1968; these were serious blows to the idealism and youthful optimism of the early sixties.

In 1969, as tensions peaked between nuclear-armed superpowers, the distinguished historian, Arnold Toynbee wrote:

It is already becoming clear that a chapter which had a Western beginning will have to have an Indian ending if it is not to end in the self-destruction of the human race. At this extremely danger-ous moment in human history, the only way of salvation for mankind is the Indian way... Here we have the attitude and the spirit that can make it possible for the human race to grow together into a single family – and, in the Atomic Age, this is the only alter-native to destroying ourselves.[2]

During the late sixties the war in South East Asia escalated rap-idly, inciting demonstrations across the US and Europe. The Civil Rights movement in the US began by following the example of Gandhi and the principle of passive resistance, but it soon turned violent. Civil unrest, riots, and demonstrations shook the pillars of society. Drugs, and the powerful sound of amplified music, added a high octane catalyst to a decade of social change. Many of the younger generation rejected some of the ideals and sexual mores of their parents. Untethered from the restraints of their traditions, many were set adrift in a sea of confusion without a compass. Many individuals and society as a whole paid a high price for their experimentation. Some took psychedelic drugs and experienced a 'stolen glimpse' of a change in consciousness – an expanded awareness that came without the preparation or work needed to allow the experience to be useful. Many sought to repeat the experience and suffered disorientation and alienation. During this decade of international tensions, civil strife, social change, and radical experimentation, some began to look for a 'way' – a path toward spiritual fulfillment.

In 1960, in London, Maharishi Mahesh Yogi introduced the practice of Transcendental Meditation to the West. Today, medita-tion is a household word, but at the time it was hardly known. If it was mentioned at all it was considered an odd practice, 'contem-plating one's navel', something a hermit did in a cave; it had little relevance to men and women engaged in worldly pursuits. That meditation, relatively unknown in Western civilization, could become practiced so widely in less than fifty years was in great part the work of three men: the Maharishi Mahesh Yogi, Dr Francis Roles, and Leon MacLaren.

From time to time during the twentieth century teachers from the East came to the West in an attempt to plant the seeds of Eastern philosophy. These seeds did not fall on fertile soil. But when the Maharishi met Dr Roles and Leon MacLaren he met two groups that had been working selflessly for decades. Maharishi had spent years in seclusion and had renounced property and position. He was not sophisticated in the ways of the West, and he had little experience with promotion, organization, or funding. He arrived in Europe without wealth or reputation, but he came with a purpose, a deep inner peace and a method of meditation shaped by his teacher Gurudeva, that he called Transcendental Meditation. This did not require sitting in a difficult cross-legged position, a monastic setting, or withdrawal from society, but could be practiced by men and women who were engaged in the affairs of community and family.

> Wherever he went he carried with him a blissful presence, smiles and laughter, and a handful of flowers that inspired the phrase 'Flower Power' – the phrase that gave a name to the 'Spirit of the Sixties'. His simple theory was that the mind would turn naturally toward the source of its own being if it is shown a simple technique. Happiness, energy, creativity, and love could be tapped from this simple means.[3]

He met Dr Roles and initiated him into the practice of meditation. Dr Roles told his group, 'This is a valid method to remember Oneself.' Dr Roles introduced Leon MacLaren to Maharishi and members of both groups were initiated. As the men and woman of the School of Economic Science and the Study Society were people of means and experience in worldly affairs, they provided the organization, meeting places, promotion, and funds he needed to establish meditation in London and then in other parts of Europe.

In the first year or two the groups grew and worked in close cooperation. Then one evening, Maharishi arranged a meeting in London. It was attended by people from his own following, the

Study Society, and the School. He suggested that the three groups, which already shared a common purpose, merge into one. He wanted Leon MacLaren to administer a worldwide organization for promoting Transcendental Meditation, and Dr Roles to travel the world as an 'Initiator', introducing people to meditation. This would have required both men to give up the leadership of their respective organizations.

Following some discussion, the lights were dimmed, and all meditated. After the meditation there arose a clear consensus. The groups would continue to work for their common aim, but each would continue to operate under the direction of their respective leaders – the Maharishi, Leon MacLaren, and Dr Roles.* The two London groups set up The School of Meditation in London, under the direction of Bill Whiting, while Maharishi went to America on to an extended world tour, building an organization.

In 1968 Maharishi traveled to India with the Beatles, Donovan, Mia Farrow and other personalities. Photo images of an Indian guru sitting cross-legged with long-haired rock stars and beautiful women attracted much attention and were widely published. In interviews, each of the four Beatles spoke of their trip to India and their impression of the Maharishi. They described how Mantra Meditation quieted the mind and gave them a sense of well-being.

In a series of televised and print interviews, the biggest stars in the entertainment industry discussed Mantra Meditation and Eastern Mysticism, while the Maharishi was interviewed on national TV talk shows. All this publicity meant that meditation became a popular topic in the media. A cartoon appeared in *Playboy* magazine depicting a couple having cocktails at a party. The caption read, 'No, I don't want to know your very own secret mantra.' In *Annie Hall*, an award-winning movie written by Woody Allen, a character at a phone booth is overheard saying, 'I forgot my Mantra.'

---

* The account of this meeting at Colet House in London was provided by Cedric and Evelyn Grigg and Mrs Shirley Burch, who were at the meeting.

All this publicity generated interest in meditation. One talk which the Maharishi gave at the Albert Hall in London attracted over four thousand people. The event was mentioned in *A Day in the Life*, a song recorded by the Beatles: 'Now we know how many wholes it takes to fill the Albert Hall.' People were attracted from all sectors of society. Men in three-piece business suits and ladies in long dresses sat next to blue collar workers, long-haired men, and woman wearing tie-dyed blouses, mini-skirts, and beads.

During the next twenty-five years, millions of people were introduced to meditation. Along the way the teacher who had lived a life of renunciation and owned nothing became the leader of a billion dollar organization, living at times in a 'Peace Palace'. The organization established a university and a political party that ran a third party candidate for the presidency of the US. Some of his followers attempted to levitate. The original impulse appeared to mutate, but there can be no doubt that meditation had been introduced to the West.

BABA MUKTANANDA
(1908–1982)

Relinquish appearances, for they are illusion.
Relinquish the turmoil of the world, for it is perishable.*

You are the seer, the seen, and the process of seeing; the creator, the creation, and the act of creating; the knower, the knowledge, and the process of knowing; the meditator, the object of meditation, and the act of meditating.†

12

Swami Muktananda

Growing Roses in Concrete

S WAMI MUKTANANDA worked independently from the other teachers whose stories are told in this book. He was a master teacher who introduced meditation to people on five continents, teaching the ancient Indian tradition and philosophy of Vedanta in an *ashram* setting as it has been taught for thousands of years in India.

When one attends a meeting at a Gurdjieff group, The Study Society, or The School, one enters a familiar Western setting. People meet in a school, a lecture hall, or a living room. They sit in chairs and listen to a lecture and a group discussion. Visiting one of Muktananda's *ashrams* one steps into the sights, sounds, and customs of an ancient tradition. Muktananda's closest disciples take up the life of a monk. They wear orange robes, take vows of celibacy, renounce worldly pursuits; they become the teachers, leading groups in chanting, meditation, and study. The inner circle is surrounded by a group of committed devotees who are householders with families and professions. They tend to the organization and administrative affairs. Many open their homes to meetings for meditation in towns and cities around the world. Visiting an *ashram* anywhere in the world one is immersed in Indian culture and tradition. One sees orange robes, saris, shrines to Indian Gods, teachers and disciples meditating in a cross-legged position, the sound of chanting, and the scent of incense. The form is foreign to many but the power of the meditation, the chanting, and the inspiration of Muktananda and his successor, Gurumayi, attracted a worldwide following.

Swami Muktananda was born in 1908 into a wealthy family in India. He left his home to begin his spiritual quest at the age of fifteen. After many years as a wandering mendicant he became a disciple of Bhagawan Nityananda. In 1947 he withdrew to a hermitage and spent eight years meditating in solitude. After teaching for years, he left India and traveled to the West. In 1970 he arrived in California where he was introduced to the 'flower generation' by Richard Alpert, PhD.

Dr Alpert was infamous, along with two other Harvard professors, Dr Timothy Leary and Dr Ralph Melzer. Dr Leary was a research professor at Harvard's Center for Personality Research. He led a project researching the potential of psycho-activating chemicals for treating personality disorders.* The professors broke research protocol by personally experimenting with the chemicals and were dismissed by Harvard.

Leary achieved notoriety promoting the use of psychedelic chemicals that induced altered states of consciousness. His influence led many toward drug abuse and alienation, and to the dismay of legitimate researchers led to the banning of all research with LSD and other psychedelic chemicals which some scientists believed had the potential to be a powerful and effective therapeutic tool. President Nixon called Leary 'the most dangerous man in America'.

Dr Alpert's message was: 'Once you get the message, hang up'.

---

* The chemicals being researched were mescaline, derived from a cactus called peyote that grows in the south western deserts of the USA and had been written about by Aldous Huxley in *The Doors of Perception*, psilocybin, derived from a South American mushroom, and Lysergic acid diethylamide (LSD), derived from ergot of rye, which had been developed by Sandos Laboratories, a Swiss pharmaceutical company, for treatment of behavioral disorders. The early researchers called these non-addictive chemicals 'psycho-activating agents'. They came to be called 'psychedelics'.

He turned his attention to Indian philosophy and meditation. He traveled across India and returned renamed as Ram Dass; he wrote several books including *Be Here Now*.* Writing and lecturing to the 'flower generation', he pointed many in the direction of meditation, yoga, and Eastern philosophy.

When Muktananda arrived in California, he caught the wave of media attention being given to meditation and Indian philosophy. Through many years of spiritual discipline, Muktananda had developed a spiritual force with the ability to transmit that force to others. His charisma and wisdom attracted a large following. He established the SYDA Foundation to administer the work of teaching meditation and Vedanta philosophy around the globe. During the next twelve years he attracted a worldwide following, establishing *ashrams* and meditation centers in cities in over thirty countries. By his death in 1982 *ashrams* and meditation centers had been established on five continents.[1]

He took up residence each summer in a large *ashram* he built in South Fallsburg, New York. Every summer, people were drawn to him from around the world and each weekend thousands of visitors came to the *ashram* to hear him speak and participate in a program of meditation and chanting. He began each talk with a bow and a greeting, 'With great respect and love, I welcome you all with all my heart'. He taught a philosophy of devotion and Self-discovery:

> Man goes to great trouble to acquire knowledge of the material world. He learns all branches of mundane science. He explores the earth and even travels to the moon. But he never tries to find what exists within himself. Because he is unaware of the enormous power that lies within him, he looks for support in the outer world. Because he doesn't know the boundless happiness that lies inside the heart, he looks for satisfaction in mundane activities

* * *

* *Be Here Now* sold over 2.5 million copies. Ram Dass' editor was Toinette Lippe, one of a small group that worked with Joy Dillingham (see Chapter 16) to establish the NY School of Practical Philosophy. She once arranged a meeting between Ram Dass and Joy who told him his encouraging the use of psychedelic drugs was a disservice to his followers.

and pleasures. Because he doesn't experience the inner love he looks for love from others. The truth is that the Inner Self of every human being is supremely great and supremely lovable. Everything is contained in the Self. The creative power of this entire universe lives inside every one of us. The Divine Principle which creates and sustains this world pulsates within us as our own Self. It scintillates in the heart, and shines through our senses. If, instead of pursuing knowledge of the outer world we were to pursue inner knowledge, we would discover that effulgence very soon.[2]

I attended one of Muktananda's last weekend 'intensives' in New York. For two days seven hundred people sat on the carpeted floor of a large meditation hall to listen to talks by Muktananda and his monks, to chant, and to meditate. Baba, as he was called, said the teacher will set before the devotee the True, the Real, and the Beautiful, but the devotee must reach out and embrace it. He must open his heart and allow the Teaching to enter. Later one of the monks told a story.

I had received a letter from a friend who was suffering from a skin condition that was not responding to treatment. He thought that if I could send him something that Baba had handled, perhaps the energy from the master could help with the healing. Walking by the garden I saw Baba sitting quietly with a few people. As I approached and sat down on the ground Baba smiled. It seemed at times Baba read one's thoughts. He took off his glasses, took a tissue, cleaned his glasses, then balled it up between his palms, smiled, and dropped it at my feet. There it was! What my friend had asked for. Then I hesitated, perhaps it was not appropriate for me to pick it up. Before I could decide another monk snatched the tissue and got up and walked away. Baba sighed; he took off his glasses, took another tissue, cleaned his glasses again, balled up the tissue between his palms and threw it at my feet. I grabbed it and went off to mail it to my friend. That is our dilemma, what we want may appear before us and we can be hesitant, bound by habit and indecision. When what the Higher Self wants is in front of you, do not hesitate; seize the moment!

At the culmination of the weekend Muktananda stepped in front of each meditator to give 'Shaktipat'. This meant that through a life devoted to spiritual practice, Muktananda had connected to an energy that could be passed on to others. He held a large bouquet of peacock's feathers with which he tapped each person on the head. He stepped in front of me, our eyes met and I bowed my head. I am not prone to imagination or hallucination but when the feathers touched my head the effect was electric; a flash of blue lightning filled my mind. Having no explanation for what had happened, I accepted what was said – I had received a profound impulse from a Master Teacher.

During the two day 'intensive' a man sat behind me who was unlike the others around us, for he was a large black man whose presence was intimidating. At the end of the weekend people were asked to speak about what had been experienced. The man behind me stood up and said, 'I have never been to anything like this. I have never even heard of anything like this. On Thursday I was sitting on a stoop in Harlem, a friend stopped by and asked me how I was and I said, "I feel like my soul is dying." My friend returned later. "Do you trust me, Joe?" he asked, and he gave me an envelope, saying, "There is a ticket in there. Go to the address on 86th Street tomorrow at 3 o'clock, and pack a change of clothes. Get on the bus; it will take you to a special place for the weekend. Just go along with the program, it will save your soul."'

He paused, then said: 'I am happy I came.'

At the end of the summer, I was visiting the *ashram*. Standing in line, I heard a familiar voice and, when I turned, it was Joe. I was struck by the change: gone was the intimidating presence.

'Hello,' I said, 'I sat in front of you during the intensive.'

He smiled. 'I remember,' he said.

I smiled, 'How is your soul?'

His smile got bigger, 'Just fine,' he said.

One of the *ashram* programs made a strong impression. Disciples went into penitentiaries to teach meditation to hardened criminals. When they began they encountered resistance from the Department of Corrections, but there was an embarrassing statistic. The rate of recidivism is over seventy-five percent, two out of three released inmates are arrested and return to prison within three years. Put simply, the prison programs designed to help criminals change their behavior are not very effective. After a few years the statistical pattern clearly showed that inmates that had learned to meditate had a much better rate of successfully returning to society.

One evening, just before Muktananda was to speak in the large hall, eight men escorted by a guard with a holstered pistol entered the hall. They had received special permission from the prison warden to visit the teacher before his return to India. It turned out to be his last visit to the US. They sat for the talk and the program, and then each approached the Guru to receive a blessing and a few words before returning to prison. I looked at each man as he walked by me on the way out of the hall. Each face was lit up with happiness and hope.

'My God,' I thought, 'he's growing roses in concrete!'

SHANTANANDA SARASWATI
(1913–1997)

Shantananda Saraswati devoted over thirty years passing on the Teaching to the West. Near the end of his life he wrote a letter to students in the West saying: 'You have all that is needed to carry on, you need only to put what has been given into practice.'

Photograph used with the kind permission of Joy Dillingham.

13

Shantananda Saraswati

I N INDIA, Shri Gurudeva passed on in 1953, the same year that Leon MacLaren and Dr Roles met in London. In his handwritten will he named Shantananda Saraswati to be his successor. Gurudeva's wisdom was universally acknowledged and his disciples and devotees were pleased that the seat of wisdom that had been empty for 165 years prior to Gurudeva's appointment would be filled for another generation. However, the selection of Shantananda Saraswati was without precedent, for though a Brahmin who met all the requirements to be Gurudeva's successor (see page 51), he had taken 'the road less traveled'.

In India there have been many *siddhas** who are revered and worshipped. Most had traveled the path of renunciation that began at an early age. The decision to forsake a worldly life and devote oneself to the pursuit of wisdom and spiritual fulfillment usually came at adolescence. Marriage and profession were sacrificed as the aspirant sought a teacher, an *ashram*, or a hermitage that he might embrace a spiritual life without distraction.

There is another path. The *siddhas* attract many householders as devotees. They come regularly for guidance and inspiration, but they remain engaged in the affairs of the world. They marry, have

---

* *Siddha* – one who is a perfected soul and master teacher of meditation, and the way to realization of unity with Brahman.

families, businesses, and professions. They are active members contributing to their communities. Later in life some of these men elect an option available in the Indian culture and enter the 'fourth stage of life'.

They put their business affairs in order, make arrangements for the care of family members, and don the orange robe of the monk. They renounce name, property, and position and take up a celibate life devoted to prayer, study, meditation, and spiritual discipline. Many contemplate this course; only a few actually take the step. Initially, their families may attempt to dissuade them for the simple reason that they will be missed. If he is firm in his resolve, his decision is respected, for the belief is that the aspirant's work will lead the family toward liberation and enlightenment. The aspirant's decision is also acknowledged by Indian tradition and law. During the first year of the aspirant's new life nothing at home changes. During that time he may have a change of heart and return to his home and life. After the passage of a year, his decision is acknowledged by the family and the community.

A ceremony is held, a funeral pyre is lit and the life of the householder is deemed to be over. Then his property is distributed according to his will. His licenses and professional entitlements expire. Under the law, the legal entity renounced by the aspirant has passed on. If after these events, the aspirant should have a change of heart and seek to return home, he does so with no right to the property or position of his former self.

Shantananda Saraswati became a devotee of Gurudeva at an early age. He wanted to become a monk but was instructed by his teacher, Gurudeva, to marry. He lived the life of a householder, worked as a bookbinder, and supported a wife and child for fourteen years. After his wife died he asked and received permission from Gurudeva to enter 'the fourth stage of life'.[1] No other man who has risen to fill the role of Shankaracharya has traveled this road. This break in tradition caused some controversy and dissent among Gurudeva's disciples.

Shantananda Saraswati was remarkable even by Shankara-charya standards. A man of great wisdom, power, and goodness, his wisdom was grounded in the experience of a householder. This made him uniquely qualified to provide spiritual wisdom and practical guidance to the masses and to be a channel for wisdom from the East to the West. That part of his story is told in Chapters 14 and 15.

Man's real nature is knowledge, truth, and bliss. No man is devoid of this, but it can be covered over. Sometimes, when one is in an agitated situation he will pick up the wrong thing although the right things are all around him. He forgets the real and gets something else for the real. This is how the eternal is replaced by the transient; it is due to ignorance and agitation. But in the consciousness is the power to discriminate between the real and unreal. That power resides in the stillness of Myself. When one is attentive and still one finds that pure 'I' emerges out of the mass of impure 'Is'. This will facilitate proper action in one's everyday work. It is a manifestation of meditation in action. This is good.

Quote from conversation between Shantananda Saraswati and Dr Roles, preserved by The Study Society.

Dr Francis C. Roles
(1901–1982)

The realization of your individual Self is done through the heart. You can't reach it through the head. You realize the nature of the Self, which is always there, but that is only half the thing. This consciousness, the Atman, then has to realize it is one with the Creator, the Self of the universe; and that is done through the mind. So you observe the laws governing the universe and the universal consciousness behind these laws. The way in is through the heart, the way out is through the mind.

Quote from *Voyage of Discovery*.
Photo published with permission of the Study Society.

14

Dr Francis Roles

Return to the Source

'ALL YOUR WORRIES are over.'[1] This opening statement was made by Dr Roles to his group in London upon returning from India in 1961. He had traveled with Maharishi to devote an intense period to meditation and self-examination. He had hoped to establish an awareness of himself. He and many of the seventy fellow travelers became sick with dysentery for several weeks and so the journey had not gone according to plan. He had told his group in London he would be back on a specific date. As the allotted time expired, he grew disappointed, for he had not accomplished the purpose of his journey. Maharishi advised him to extend his stay; Dr Roles was reluctant to do so, as he had said he would return on a specific date. He and his teacher Ouspensky had lived by the maxim, 'A man's word is his bond'. Maharishi urged him to send a telegram to London. He said Dr Roles had not accomplished his aim, and there was another reason.

Maharishi had just returned from a visit with Shantananda Saraswati, who had by then succeeded Gurudeva as the Shankaracharya of the North. Though Maharishi and Shantananda Saraswati had both been disciples of Gurudeva, Maharishi was a bit nervous about the audience, being uncertain about how the new head of the order would respond to his work in the West. All went well. Indeed, he was given praise, encouragement and guidance. On learning that the Shankaracharya was coming to visit Maharishi and his London guests, Dr Roles finally sent the telegram.

On the day of his arrival Shantananda Saraswati was received with great pomp and ceremony. There had been days of preparation. Dr Roles observed that amidst the great fanfare, ringing of bells, gongs, and blowing of conch shells, Shantananda Saraswati remained unmoved. He brought to the large gathering of excited devotees a powerful presence that radiated calm and bliss. Dr Roles said, 'When I first saw him arrive at the gates of Ram Nagar, I recognized that here at last was the embodiment of Self-remembering.'[2]

'He is the only man I ever met that, whatever the circumstances, always remembers himself.'[3]

During the meetings that followed, Maharishi introduced Dr Roles and his group to the Shankaracharya as the people in London who made his work possible. The Shankaracharya was generous and encouraged questions. During one of his responses he proclaimed that 'All the difficulties arise when we fail to remember our self.'[4] These words had a profound effect on Dr Roles, as they were the very ones used by Ouspensky in 1947 during one of their last conversations fourteen years previously. He had fulfilled his instruction. He had 'returned to the source'.

Shantananda Saraswati continued: 'The whole thing is we never remember ourselves. All our troubles come from not remembering ourselves, only we can't talk about this because it is not understood.' He told a story to illustrate this:

> Ten men were sitting on the bank of the Ganges River. They decided to swim across to the other side. On the way over they got nervous because of the current, so when they came to the other side they began to count heads. They counted up and to their horror found there were only nine and, whoever counted, the answer was always nine for the tenth man was the man who was counting and he had forgotten to count himself. They grew so distraught they

began to prepare a funeral. At that point a wise man passing by reminded the one counting to remember himself.

This is difficult to understand. It is as if each of us possessed two houses. One is small and dark with little in it and bars on the windows and in that house we choose to live most of our lives. We forget that we also possess a magnificent house filled with everything we could want. If only we could remember that we owned this larger house we would not be content to live in the small house all the time.[5]

Before he returned to London Dr Roles had a private audience with the Shankaracharya, who answered questions and offered insight and direction for the work in London. Dr Roles asked if he could return and see him and received the reply, 'I have been waiting for you.'[6] (Dr Roles told this to several people, but it is not in the record.) Shantananda Saraswati ended the meeting by saying; 'I will be here the same time next year.' Thus began a relationship between the master teacher and Dr Roles that lasted until Dr Roles passed on in 1982 and continued with other members of The Study Society for the remainder of Shantananda Saraswati's life.

Dr Roles was now connected to the ancient Vedanta Tradition based on meditation and the philosophy of Advaita. It states that the Divine is eternally present in every individual and to quote Dr Roles, 'Your own Self that lives in the hearts of all is exactly the same as the Consciousness that creates and sustains the Universe.'[7] The Work is to realize that unity, the first step is to experience it; a Work Dr Roles realized and taught until his death.

Dr Roles once said:

The meditation is half of the business; that, as the mystics say, you give up all of your willing and thinking, and then you will hear the truth. That is half of it. The rest of your life you have to be somebody of good thinking and good will, otherwise you get into frightful trouble! If you meditate and then go and think nasty things about people I am told God does not like it.[8]

Dr Roles assured his group that there was no conflict between the 'System' that had been elucidated by Gurdjieff and Ouspensky and the Vedanta Tradition that was being illuminated by Shantananda Saraswati. They stemmed from the same ancient tradition. In their conversations the Shankaracharya spoke of the Fourth Way. He spoke about the Law of Seven, the Law of Three, the mind, heart, and instinct of men and other fundamental principles they had been studying in the System. He was certain he had found in India a 'Fourth Way School'. He believed the meditation was one of the missing fragments for which they had been searching. And they had found in Shantananda Saraswati one who had realized the full potential of a human being, a man who remembered himself and lived in conscious identity with the Absolute.

The Shankaracharya was asked why this knowledge had not produced more results. He said, 'Every spiritual truth, however simple, is at once distorted when it reaches an unrealized person.' He told a story to illustrate this:

> A man went to a teacher and asked him about God, and the teacher said, I will answer your question in the simplest possible way, in three words, 'God is everywhere'. Well satisfied, the man went away. Going along the road he saw an elephant coming toward him with a rider on his back and he thought to himself, God is everywhere, God is in the elephant, God is in me. Can God harm God? I will walk straight on. When he got a little nearer the rider asked him to move out of the way, and then shouted at him, but the man said, no, God is in the elephant, God is in me, I am going on. When he reached the elephant, the elephant took him in his trunk and tossed him across the road where he landed much shaken and bruised. When he had recovered a little, he hobbled back to the teacher and said, 'I have been trying to act according to what you said and look what happened.' The teacher asked him to recount what had happened, and the man told the story. The teacher said, 'You should understand fully before you begin to act. It is right that God is in everything; God is in you, God is in the elephant, but God is also in the rider. He told you to get out of the way, and you disobeyed and suffered the consequences.'[9]

Truth can only be passed on to the degree of understanding of the listener. Over time it is distorted, as knowledge is passed from generation to generation, the conscious impulse of a master teacher is diluted. This was fully understood by Ouspensky. Dr Roles also understood when he received the instruction to 'return to the source'.

Dr Roles met his wife, Joan, while a student at Cambridge; they remained devoted to one another for the rest of their lives. She assisted and supported him in every aspect of the work. She traveled with him in 1972, participated in the conversations with the Shankaracharya, and accompanied him on his last visit in 1976. On that last visit she asked the teacher about the parable of the wedding garment (Mathew 22: 11-14) and preparing for death. He answered:

> You have already been betrothed and you needn't think about such things at all. You have been visiting this future wedding place every day during your meditation. Your union is already established. When death, which has to come to all of us, comes, all one has to keep in mind is that this body is being discarded... the only advice to be given is to shed all feelings of fear of going into the unknown, to remain aware that the loss of body is not a loss in any way. You have performed the deeds the body has to perform in the best way and there it ends. The future journey is going to be all right for you.[10]

In July of 1981 Joan slipped into a coma, her breathing stopped and she appeared to pass but then she revived. She opened her eyes with a radiant smile and whispered, 'Tell them it's OK for everyone in the end.'[11]

Joan passed on shortly thereafter. After fifty-four years of marriage, Dr Roles managed to let his wife die safely in their own home and in her own bed. He remained positive and happy throughout the entire experience of his wife's departure.[12]

In June of 1982, after a long and happy day spent with family and friends in his home, Dr Roles said, 'Everything I have had to do has now been done. The need is for simplicity. We have been habitually complicating everything. It is only necessary to be quiet and keep things simple. There is only one consciousness. The levels of consciousness are impediments to that Universal Consciousness. Everything is that Consciousness. That is what we have to feel and know.' He died a few hours later on June 11, 1982.[13]

For his obituary his son-in-law read a quote from *I Am That*:

> He becomes nonexistent like a river becomes nonexistent when it merges into the sea. Its name and form are lost but the water remains and is one with the sea. His goodness, wisdom, vitality, become the heritage of mankind, and help the development of everyone and everything. His immortal thoughts, his spirit of service and sacrifice, his selfless dedication, his acute sensitiveness for the welfare of others have become our heritage: vital, vibrant, and shining, like a kindly light in the darkness.[14]

His students carried on, continuing to have audiences with Shantananda Saraswati until 1993. He died in 1997. The groups in New York, London, Mexico, Australia, and other locations study the words of the master and continue with the Work. They have published a number of books based on the conversations with the master teacher they call 'His Holiness'.*

---

* The Study Society in New York and London have published a number of books containing extracts from the conversations with Shantananda Saraswati and the stories he told: *Good Company* I and II, *The Orange Book*, *The Man Who Wanted to Meet God*, *Birth and Death* and *The Teachings of His Holiness Shantananda Saraswati*.

SITARAM JAISWAL
(1923-2013)

The Truth is that which exists, has existed, and will exist: phys-
ically, intellectually, or emotionally. And it exists by virtue of the
Will of the Absolute. It is called constant – that which remains
the same, does not change. So whatever exists, the truth of that
existence can never change. The substance, the object, may
change, but the truth about that substance, that object, will never
change. That remains the truth, because it has been manifested
by the most powerful, ever-prevailing force we call consciousness, or the Absolute. Some prefer to call it God... but that is a
matter of linguistic choice. Substance is the same, whether you
call it consciousness, or God, or Brahman.*

The system of *mantra* has evolved to train the mind to be attentive, to be serious, to be purposeful. The mantra is a device to
train the mind so it doesn't do unnecessary things.†

* Adapted from London lecture, 2001.
† Adapted from London lecture, 2006.

15

Satsanga

Good Company

I N 1965 Dr Roles traveled to India to arrange a meeting between Shantananda Saraswati and Leon MacLaren. The audience took place in his *ashram* in the busy city of Allahabad. The sounds of the city could be easily heard. Mr MacLaren entered the room to find Shantananda Saraswati sitting on a dais cross-legged, eyes closed in meditation. A profound peace and sense of well-being filled the room; next to him sat the translator, Mr Jaiswal, an Indian who had spent many years in London. He translated from both the Hindi and Sanskrit. Shantananda Saraswati opened his eyes and spoke:

> It is not my desire which has to be carried out. The desire, which has to be helped, is that which arises in people looking for the truth, wishing to acquire the divine life, and to make efforts in that direction; and so far as I can, I will always be ready. My door is always open to anyone, known or unknown, Eastern or Western, irrespective of his upbringing or culture, because in fact we all come from the same stock. As long as that desire and the decision are strong, permanent, and stable, the help will always be available.[1]

So began a relationship between the Shankaracharya of the North and Leon MacLaren and the School that lasted until the

Shankaracharya's passing in 1997. Dr Roles and other leaders, including Mr Whiting of the School of Meditation, also came to Allahabad to spend a week or more having daily audiences with the man they called His Holiness. They came with their questions, and to report on The Work in the West, and they received wisdom, inspiration, and guidance. The Shankaracharya advised them on meditation, illumined the scriptures – both Eastern and Western – and provided guidance on spiritual practice. He drew on his own life experience to offer advice on every aspect of life: marriage, child rearing, principles of education, ethics in the work place, diet, and health. He taught them to develop their spiritual life while fully engaged in worldly responsibilities, encouraging them to act to uplift their families, professions and communities, and to manifest the harmony, beauty, and efficiency of their spiritual practices in their everyday life.

Commenting on this, Donald Lambie, a barrister by profession who succeeded Leon MacLaren as the leader of the School of Economic Science in 1994 remarked: 'In the course of history there are significant events. When these men met, it was important.'[2] The course of human events was altered, the ancient wisdom of India was made available to Western Civilization.

The Shankaracharya spoke Hindi and Sanskrit. The conversations were translated into English by Sitaram Jaiswal, who was of Indian origin but had spent many years in England. He was fluent in Hindi and English, and a student of Sanskrit. He had worked with both Dr Roles and Leon MacLaren. His knowledge of the two cultures, as well as their traditions and scriptures, made him uniquely qualified to translate these conversations as well as Shantananda Saraswati's correspondence with the West. Jaiswal once said,

> The West is fundamentally individualistic, the East has been universalist. The individualism of the West has led to great material and technological advances. In the East the universalists have also achieved great things. They have expounded the philosophy of *Advaita* which brings you to oneness. This 'oneness' contains

everything. But being universalist or being individualistic is not the ultimate answer of human life or human aspiration, the real purpose of our life is to be free in every respect.[3]

That a man of understanding with such a unique background and language skills was available to facilitate the transmission of knowledge from East to West could lead one to believe in Providence.

When Shantananda Saraswati retired as Shankaracharya and withdrew from public life, it was Jaiswal who asked him to continue to provide access and guidance to members of the Study Society and the School Economic Science.[4]

When in India, Jaiswal and his wife lived with Shantananda Saraswati. During the last years of his life, when his health was failing, Mrs Jaiswal cared for him. At one point Mrs Jaiswal, who was an attorney, saw a great need in the area of children's education and she and her husband decided to establish a school for primary education. They were able to gather the funds and talent to open a school but encountered an obstacle. When Jaiswal presented the applications for the new school the city officials would not issue the permits without a bribe. Unwilling to taint a pure impulse with a dishonest act he did not pay the bribes. His application was denied. Undaunted and confident that the good would prevail he submitted his application every year for fifteen years; being denied or ignored each year. The fifteenth year the application came to the attention of an honest official who cut through the corruption and the inertia and issued the permits. The Mukularanyam School was established and flourished. It is thriving today.[5]

Jaiswal visited New York many times, he brought to us the wisdom of the master teacher and carried with him a profound goodness and the essence of *Advaita* philosophy (non-dualism). He did not consider himself Indian or English. He did not think of us as Americans. He lived many years with Shantananda Saraswati and acknowledged one Self in all he met. Speaking to students in

New York in 1998 he said, 'It is not our business to make Hindus of Christians, or Christians of Hindus … The religion of your birth is a gift from the Absolute. There is great value in these traditions, you would be wise to practice your religion.'

The conversations with Shantananda Saraswati were recorded and transcribed. The leaders brought back this wisdom to their groups where it was studied, practiced, and actualized in the lives of many. MacLaren wrote the material for philosophy courses that were offered to the public. He was able to express this ancient teaching in a way that was accessible to the Western mind; a teaching that taught men and women to lead a life that included meditation, self-examination, and study; a teaching that enabled them to lead measured, fruitful lives earning a living and support-ing families, while engaging in the highest of spiritual pursuits. This echoed the inscription above the entrance at the Temple of Delphi, 'Know Thy Self' and 'Nothing in Excess'. Such a life reveals that one's true Self is the underlying consciousness, the Self of All.

During an off the record conversation with MacLaren, Shantananda Saraswati described with great sadness the 'frozen' condition in India. He said the center for spirituality had shifted from India to the West.[6]

During the next decade MacLaren's students established Philosophy Schools and schools for educating children in Europe, the United States, Canada, the Caribbean, New Zealand, Australia and South Africa. His vision was vast. He thought in terms of centuries. When setting up the charters for the schools he said some of these institutions would last five hundred years. He once returned to London to find that a steel beam had been installed to support a sagging school building. He had the beam removed and replaced with an oak beam. He said we know an oak support will last for 500 years; steel beams have been around less than a century.

Each year MacLaren traveled the world visiting these schools with the message: 'We come to discover the Truth, the Truth about our Self, The One Self, the One Consciousness that pervades and sustains everything. We speak the truth, we strive to live according to the truth.' He would visit each school for several weeks. He was tireless, even during the last years when his health was failing. On one of his last visits to New York, he arrived at 3:00 pm and held a meeting at 5:30 pm. Having traveled from Australia through Los Angeles, he quipped it had been a long time since an angel had visited the city! He spoke to us for over an hour. The body was weak, but he himself knew no limits. He brought us the inspiration he had received from Shantananda Saraswati. MacLaren's words, presence, and example provided an annual impulse:

For this inner change, this development, to take place the knowledge, we have been given must be put into practice. There is a time factor in this Work; it is the number of times the knowledge is put into practice. These are the pulses in the life. The important things are to lead a measured life, to meditate, and the increasing use of the power to rest in the awareness of One Self while engaged in practical affairs. At first that seems very difficult, but keep moving and you will find it is not so difficult, and one day it becomes a steady-state, one just rests while one moves about the world, and then the being begins to fill with light, and you step into the first stable stage that death cannot remove. In this way one moves forward. It is up to you whether you meditate; it is up to you whether you keep the measures; it is up to you whether you rest in the awareness of my Self; no one can do it for you.

The mind has to be cleansed of all this rubbish; to learn not to dwell on random circling thoughts and learn to rest in the awareness of my Self. It will become easier to let what is arising in the mind pass without being troubled by it, so that one can keep moving and not be arrested as if one had a perpetual stammer. This is how it goes, cleanse the mind by replacing false ideas with true ones; observe, measure, meditate; put what you know into practice, particularly making use of the power to rest in the awareness of my Self, and letting the movements of the mind just pass, as is their nature, without clinging to them and dwelling on them. The nature of the spirit is such that, if you work, you will keep moving, keep refining. You will become people of consequence and of use to the whole of humanity, each in your own way; this will surely happen, and humanity is in sore need, but it does not take that many to meet that need.

So that is what we have to do; not just live for our little selves, but remember that all we receive... the knowledge, the meditation, and indeed the power that comes from our own Self... all this is for the Self, which means it is for everyone. Always remember that. That is what it is about and that is how we move, and the human spirit will certainly flow on... do not settle for anything less than the ocean, keep moving.

So ladies and gentlemen, let us pause... rest in the awareness of my Self, the one Self of us all, and let us dedicate all we receive and all our work to the service of Truth...[7]

He taught until the last week of his life. In 1994, though ill, he flew from London to South Africa to lead a study week with the School's senior students. His visit was cut short when his health failed. He was flown back to London, where he died.

Girl with the Lamp of Wisdom, Walkill, New York.
Bronze by Nathan David.

16

Joy Dillingham and Nicolai Rabeneck

Guarding the Light

The growth and development of philosophy schools, work groups, study societies, and centers for meditation, around the world is an extraordinary phenomenon. They arise and develop in response to an essential need to find answers to the fundamental questions of life. What am I? What is the nature of the Creation? What is one's relationship to the creation and the Creator? When people desire the truth, a school or group will grow to meet the demand. These groups arise, develop, and are founded on universal principles. Conditions in different countries and cultures differ, but the principles are universal. And so the stories of these schools and groups are similar. I witnessed the growth and development of The New York School of Practical Philosophy. It is a story, versions of which have been repeated all over the world.

Leon MacLaren said, 'When no man steps forward to meet a need, a woman will.' He believed that conditions in New York City would make the establishment of a School there as challenging as in any city in the world. That task fell to a woman.

Joy Dillingham graduated from the University of Washington and won a Fulbright Scholarship to the London Academy of

Music and Dramatic Art in 1956. Shortly after her arrival in London, she sought advice from the headmaster, Michael MacOwan, who introduced her to his teacher, Dr Francis Roles. Dr Roles recognized something special about the young lady and invited her to attend his group. During her education in London and on a tour with a Repertory Theater Company, she was introduced by Dr Roles and Michael MacOwan to the study of Ouspensky's 'System'.

When it was time for her to return to New York, Dr Roles offered to provide her with material to take with her to New York. She gratefully accepted and over the next few years a group of twenty-five people gathered and grew into the New York Study Society.

Dr Roles informed her that Nicolai Rabeneck was somewhere in New York. Rabeneck had been with Ouspensky from the beginning in London. He was a scholar who spoke and wrote English and Russian fluently. He and his wife had overcome great difficulties to escape Russia and travel to London during the Revolution. He became Ouspensky's right hand man, assisting with his writings and translations. He was one of the few who spoke with Ouspensky in Russian, so the transmission of knowledge was direct. In 1941, after Ouspensky had moved to America, he had asked Rabeneck to find a way to join him.

It was wartime and London was being bombed, but having lived through the Russian Revolution and the Depression this was not an insurmountable obstacle for such people. It took three and a half years for Rabeneck and his wife to relocate to America. He took a job in London with an eye on a transfer. After eighteen months he was transferred to Trinidad, where he worked for two years before managing to move to New York City. He spent three years working with Ouspensky in New York before Ouspensky, because of declining health, returned to London in 1947.[1]

Joy Dillingham contacted Rabeneck and they worked together for eight years. They spent many evenings in his kitchen where Rabeneck recalled stories and related conversations that he had

had with Ouspensky. As Dr Roles had hoped, he worked with the Study Society for the rest of his life. Rabeneck wrote to Shantananda Saraswati with his questions and received direct guidance. I met Nicolai Rabeneck years later when he was ninety. Joy Dillingham had invited him to the Philosophy School's retreat center in upstate New York and asked me to attend to him. This was fortuitous, as I had studied everything written by Ouspensky. During the three days I spent in his company, I observed and listened closely as we conversed, hoping to gain a deeper insight into Ouspensky and his work. Rabeneck was remarkable. At ninety, he was completing the writing of the introduction to the fourth printing of *Tertium Organum*, which had remained in print for seventy years; and he had resumed the study of Sanskrit under the tuition of Dillingham. His health was failing, and she was caring for him. He had been a source of knowledge for The Study Society in New York for decades. Along with Dillingham and others from The Study Society, including Tom Gerst, an American who had returned from London, Rabeneck started the group that grew into the New York School of Practical Philosophy.

One Saturday evening he addressed a group of eighty people. His words and presence made an impression that lives with me today. But my quest for an insight into Ouspensky was not satisfied. It was years later before it dawned on me: I had been focused on Ouspensky's intellect, the man who had shaped Gurdjieff's knowledge into a system. What I had overlooked was that underneath this brilliance, there was a foundation of goodness. Married and faithful to one woman, impeccably honest, his word was his bond. As mentioned before, Dr Roles once described Ouspensky as, 'the first man I met whom I could trust completely'. I had experienced that strength, kindness, and generosity firsthand in Nicolai Rabeneck. Joy Dillingham summed it up: she said he was, 'The Soul of the Work'.

In May 1976 The Study Society invited Dr Roles to New York. He gave two lectures attended by an invited audience:

NICOLAI RABENECK
(1891-1982)

The word religion means 'to relate to something'; 'to relate from the lower to the higher energies'.*

Everything is in the heart. If you feel it in the heart then there is something real behind it, and the Real is the Self, the Eternal Spark that's in everybody. Let us move together with unity, Let us finish this evening with a bright silence....†

* New York lecture, 1972.
† New York lecture, 1976.
Photograph reproduced from *The Bridge*, #12, page 142.

I will begin by introducing Mr Rabeneck to those who don't know him. He and his wife escaped Russia two years after the revolution started, and made their way to Mr Ouspensky's group in London in the thirties, shortly before my wife and I found it. We have campaigned together ever since. He had the great advantage of speaking Mr Ouspensky's language, so they had many private conversations about which I heard only later. And he made his own connection with the center of things in India. I would like everybody to know that nothing of that work could have continued in New York since Ouspensky's death in 1947, but for Mr Rabeneck. None of the material you have received these past thirty years or are going to receive, could have reached you, so I hope you are as grateful to him as I am.[2]

In 1963, Tom Gerst, a student who had attended the School of Economic Science in London for a year and a half, was returning to his home in New York City. He had been inspired in London and expressed a desire to attend a school in New York City. Mr MacLaren was traveling at the time so the school principal suggested Mr Gerst start a school. When Mr MacLaren returned, he thought the young man would need some assistance.

This was the time when the School and the Study Society in London were working closely together. Some of Dr Roles' students were teaching at the School. MacLaren's wife, Joyce, was a student of Dr Roles, and both groups were working with the Maharishi to introduce meditation. Dr Roles was the inititator for members of the Study Society and the School into the practice. One gentleman who provided background information about these years mentioned he was attending both groups each week on different evenings. When asked about his enthusiasm he smiled and explained he had a girlfriend in each group!

Through Dr Roles the Study Society in New York was enlisted to help Tom Gerst. It could be said the New York School was an offspring that grew out of the brief union in London of The School of Economic Science and The Study Society. It was Dillingham who received the request from Dr Roles. She, Rabeneck, Bill Hager, Katie Sutter, and others from the Study Society assisted Tom Gerst.

They began in 1964 by handing out printed invitations to an Adult Study Workshop. As Gerst's business required him to travel, it was Joy Dillingham who led a weekly meeting held in a cooking school in Manhattan. She used the philosophy material that had been written by Leon MacLaren.

The initial attendance was fleshed out by members of the Study Society, followed by a 'Part 2' also written by Leon MacLaren and tutored by Joy. Members of the Society padded attendance on both evenings. After eighteen months of word-of-mouth, posters, and invitations, they were attracting enough students to be self-sufficient. Dr Roles felt the task had been fulfilled and the Study Society withdrew. Joy Dillingham was inspired by the philosophy material and the contact she had with MacLaren. She liked the structured approach that appealed to a wider circle of people, so she decided to continue with the School.

This was a fortuitous decision for the New York School, and a difficult one for her. Leon MacLaren had given up a career in law and politics to lead the School of Economic Science in London. When she left the Study Society, she left behind all of her associations both personal and professional, as well as a promising career in the theater. Eight years later, in 1972, Dr Roles visited New York and gave two lectures at The Study Society. When he met her, he embraced her and, referring to her work leading the School, said: 'All was as it is intended to be.' This meant a great deal to her: she thought of Dr Roles as her first teacher. By then the School was established and attracting over six hundred new students a year. During those years she had a job as a teacher in a private school. A beautiful woman, she was a gifted teacher with a strong stage presence.

MacLaren sent her to California where she spent time with the Maharishi learning how to care for students meditating. She described him as a man, 'incapable of a negative emotion'. He was a constant source of inspiration and happiness, and as he traveled the world, the practice of Transcendental Meditation flowered all around him.

Under her leadership the group grew. In 1968 a building was purchased on West 80th Street in Manhattan. It was a five story brownstone in a neglected condition that the previous owner had divided into small rooms and used as a rooming house. She and several people who were instrumental in founding the School moved in and established their residences there.* Over the next ten years the original rooms and architectural details were repaired and restored.

A few years after the purchase of the building, the School learned this building had served as the original center for Vivekenanda's Vedanta Society. Since then the building had then been sold and passed through several owners, but now the building, which had been the center for meditation and study of Vedanta during the first decade of the twentieth century, was to serve the same purpose for the last three decades of that century.†

It took years to acquire state accreditation for the Philosophy Foundation and the day school that grew into The Philosophy Day School for children. I once asked Joy Dillingham what motivated her to make the effort to have the Philosophy Foundation accredited by the State of New York as a 'School.' She said, 'There are times when knowledge is suppressed and organizations that promote truth are threatened. When that time comes, and it surely will, the School will have the protection of the law.'

One may wonder how a philanthropic organization grows into an established institution in the center of New York City. It grows through devotion and selfless effort. Joy Dillingham often remarked, 'Prosperity is a spiritual state'. Men and women were attracted to the wisdom and practical knowledge provided by

---

* The building became the home of Joy Dillingham, John and Katherine LeMee, Olga Coolidge and Fred Helmers. The parlor floor and the rear of the garden floor were used for philosophy classes and to introduce students to meditation.
† There are 100,000 brownstones in New York City. It is difficult to dismiss as a 'coincidence' the fact that two independent organization taught Vedanta Philosophy and meditation from the same building, one at the beginning and one at the end of the twentieth century. For a more meaningful explanation, see Ouspensky's observation on the 'inner connection' on page 16, fourth paragraph.

senior students who tutored, and a supporting staff whose work and service were motivated by a love of truth and the desire to convey it to others. Prosperity and harmony with the community do not arise by accident. In all its activities the school strove to be a good neighbor and a contributing member of the community.

When Dillingham left The Study Society, the responsibility for leading the group was taken up by Bill Hager, who was assisted by Katie Sutter. They were soon married. Katie continued to serve the group for the remainder of her life and Bill Hager continues to do so. In 2010, in a conversation with me, he said, 'The purpose of The Study Society is to preserve in its purity the knowledge passed on to us by Shantanda Saraswati.'

This reflected an instruction given by Dr Roles when he visited the New York group in May, 1976:

> I came to see if the True Knowledge – the very precious knowledge, was being scattered or lost in any way. Because this knowledge, that has been entrusted to us by Shankaracharya [Shantananda Saraswati], must be kept absolutely pure. I think the chief danger is that people take little bits of the knowledge they like and forget others… That is no good for self-realization. For self-realization – for the group as a whole, or for any individual – you must have the truth, the whole truth, and nothing but the truth.[3]

To further that aim, The Study Society published books of conversations between Shantanda Saraswati and Dr Roles. Groups in many countries study the conversations, work to realize the knowledge and put it into practice in their lives.

The relationship between Leon MacLaren and Joy Dillingham was one of Platonic love and mutual respect. When he went to see Shantananda Saraswati, he sent her letters from India. She once traveled with him and a group that visited schools around the world. While touring the schools, he would send her letters from Australia, South Africa, and Europe. They corresponded and spoke regularly for thirty years.

He recognized the difficult challenge of a woman leading a

School in New York City during the turbulent sixties and seventies, and he provided encouragement and support. He visited New York for several weeks each year. Indeed, he spent more time there than any other School except London. He sent his senior students from London to New York to lecture, teach, and provide assistance. She traveled to London every other year. He was her teacher and a difficult task master, for he held her to the highest standards of discipline. He told her not to marry so as to completely devote herself to the work of the School. This was unusual as leaders of schools and groups around the world were married. She accepted the sacrifice, the discipline and the solitary life, although at times the loneliness was a heavy cross. After twenty-seven years, when the strain of leadership took its toll on her health, making it difficult for her to fulfill her role as School leader, he replaced her. Although it was not her will, she accepted it with grace and dignity, and it did not weaken the bond forged between them by thirty years of love of Truth. At the moment of his death in 1994, though five thousand miles apart, she felt it, called London, and confirmed his passing.

The students she taught for twenty-seven years carried on and the School continues to flourish. When she retired in poor health, Jaiswal and his wife invited her to live with them, and His Holiness, so that they could care for her and help restore her health. She was deeply touched by the invitation, but it did not come to pass. She retired to New Mexico, her health recovered, and she continued the Work. For seventeen years she and William Kemsley continued to teach small groups in Santa Fe, Los Alamos, and Taos, New Mexico.

It has been fifty-five years since Joy began The Study Society in New York and fifty years since the founding of the group that grew into The New York School of Practical Philosophy. Thirty-five thousand people have been introduced to a philosophy based on the wisdom of the wisest of mankind. Many have been introduced to meditation. The Philosophy Day School offered children an education with the highest of academic and moral standards, helping

JOY DILLINGHAM
(1933-)

The teacher is the 'Magic Flute' whose work is to be open and allow the notes of Truth to pass through.

You can have anything you want, you just have to accept everything that goes along with it.

We don't learn from our mistakes; get it right, practice that and then the learning begins.

You cannot know yourself through bliss alone for bliss is your very nature. You must face the opposite – what you are not. You must see the false as false to find enlightenment. Nothing physical or mental can give you freedom. You are free once you understand that your bondage is of your own making, and you cease forging the chains that bind you.

Meditation will take you all the way home.

Conversations with the author.

to raise children to serve and uplift their communities and the nation. Inspired by Leon MacLaren, philosophy schools and day schools affiliated with the School of Economic Science in London have been established on every continent and in over twenty countries.

17

Last Days

THE MANNER in which many of these teachers spent the last days of their lives is inspirational and instructive. Socrates said philosophy was the art of dying (Plato's *Phaedo*). Dr Welch said of Gurdjieff, 'I have seen many men die. He died like a king.' Although in pain for the last two years of his life, he gathered students and taught to the end, and then wrote his last message to his students by preparing the readings for his own funeral.

Ouspensky gave instructions to his group, 'To begin again, return to the source.' The instruction set the students on a course that led them to India and the guidance needed to finish his work.

Willem Nyland was in an oxygen tent, laboring for breath, when he recorded his last message to his group encouraging them to continue.

Leon MacLaren's health was failing when he flew from London to South Africa to provide one last impulse to a group of students. The visit was cut short when he grew weak. He was flown home to London where he passed on.

These teachers treated their death not as the end of the story but as the end of a chapter. They lived their lives on a world stage and played their roles well. They understood that the final act could provide a conscious impulse for others. In many cases their final act was their finest hour.

This work builds a strong bond between men. At times the bond is not terminated by death. Dr Roles reported being profoundly and directly influenced by Ouspensky after his teacher's death. Joy Dillingham, though five thousand miles away from Leon MacLaren, 'knew' the moment of his passing. Other students of these master teachers, including the author, have reported similar experiences. Shantananda Saraswati said, 'Though bodies pass on, the connection between teacher and student remains until both are liberated.' There have been times during meditation when the connection has been experienced.

Leon MacLaren was once asked by a group of doctors about treating patients who were close to death. He said it is not a disease or illness that kills the body. The body dies when the consciousness withdraws. When that happens nothing the doctor can do will preserve the life. Until then it is the duty of the physician to take measures to support the life, and take no action to terminate the life.

Western hospitals can be aggressive in their care of patients near death. Unnecessary tests and procedures are often habitually prescribed. I heard a priest speaking with a doctor about an elderly patient in the last stage of life, the priest said: 'We advise nutrition, hygiene, and hydration.'

I once spoke with a Tibetan doctor; he was the personal physician to the Dalai Lama. I asked him if his treatment of patients in the last stage of life differed from Western doctors. He said Buddhists do not view the death of the body as the end of the life, but as a transition. Thus when selecting the treatment, they would not take measures that would disrupt the transition. For example, they administer drugs for pain but would take care to leave the person conscious. The doctor said, 'The continuation of life after the death of the body is not a theory, and we act accordingly. When you get in your automobile you cannot see the road ahead or the destination but you put gas in the car and make preparations for your arrival.'

Frederick Helmers was a teacher of philosophy, an adjunct professor at Adelphi College and the New York College of Insurance.

He was one of a handful of people who gathered around Joy Dillingham in the sixties and devoted decades of their lives to establishing the New York School of Practical Philosophy.*

The first time I saw him he was at a lectern, tutoring an introductory philosophy course at the New York School – a tall, trim and handsome man with fair features, a captivating smile, blue eyes, a clear voice and lucid mind. Later I heard a number of his students from Adelphi and the College of Insurance were attracted by his presence and found their way to the School.

One such described an incident: during a pause in the classroom conversation, Fred Helmers picked up a glass, took a drink of water and returned the glass precisely to the center of the coaster. The student was struck by the way the teacher had given his full attention to this simple task. He sought out the teacher after class. The student's observation and their subsequent conversation led him to the School.

Three years after I met Fred Helmers, he was trotting across Seventy-Ninth Street to catch a bus when he noticed something was wrong with his legs. After doctors' visits and several tests he was diagnosed with multiple sclerosis. The disease progressed and he went from a cane, to crutches, to a wheel chair. The condition paralyzed his legs but left his upper body, mind, and speech unaffected. He was lucid and able to teach until the end of his life. Nonetheless, this was a difficult cross to bear. He'd been a fiercely independent man. Though he turned the head of many a lady, he never married. His body had been as strong as his mind: he had worked his way through college as a carpenter and one summer in his youth he made his way to Alaska to work on a fishing boat during the salmon run.

---

* There were others who were with Dillingham from the sixties and devoted decades of their lives to The Work and to establishing the NY Philosophy School. Among them were Toinette Lippe (editor), Olga Coolidge (teacher, and a descendent of President Coolidge), Dr Jean Le Mée (Head of the Engineering Department of Cooper Union College), his wife, Dr Katharine Le Mée (an accomplished teacher of music), Irene Woods (administrative assistant) and Allan Moller (attorney) and his wife Rita.

It's hard to imagine the difficulty of a man with a strong and independent nature accepting a physical condition that each year found him growing more dependent on others to meet his most basic needs. Though confined to a wheelchair, he continued to commute and teach at two colleges and the NY School. In fact, his teaching activities increased. He started a Plato study group that met at his residence and drew students for many years. He was a Socratic scholar that lived the philosophy he taught. By this time he had many students who were more than willing to help. Every day people visited his apartment to assist him. And each visitor met the same presence they saw in the classroom: positive, attentive to his guests, always listening without criticism or judgment. Each person who came to help received far more than they gave.

During his last weeks he was confined to a hospital. When I visited, though his body had little strength and he could barely move, I was met with the same generous spirit. In our conversation he said that although his body was no longer of any use, the identification was still strong. That evening Joy Dillingham visited. They spent the time preparing for what was soon to come. The next morning he awoke and sitting by his bed was a student, who served him a cup of tea. The teacher sipped the tea, smiled and said, 'Today is the happiest day of my life.' An hour later he closed his eyes and passed peacefully. His students continue to lead groups that study Plato.

At the entrance to the School of Practical Philosophy in New York,
on the wall is a relief created by Nathan David. It is produced in bronze
and was inspired by Ficino's description of Philosophy as a goddess
welcoming students into the garden of philosophy.

18

The Bridge

I N 1915 Gurdjieff and Ouspensky met in Russia and began the
work of introducing Eastern esoteric knowledge to the West.
This coincided with the onset of World War I and the Bolshevik
Revolution in Russia.

It was in 1960 that the Maharishi introduced Transcendental
Meditation to Europe. In 1993, the last conversations between
Shantananda Saraswati and members of the School and the Study
Society concluded the transmission of an ancient Indian tradition
of sacred knowledge to the West. During that time the world had
gone from the imminent threat of nuclear war to a world watching in amazement as the Berlin Wall was torn down, the 'Iron
Curtain' dissolved, and the 'Cold War' ended. After decades of
military confrontation in Europe, Southeast Asia, Africa, and South
America, the dissolution of the Soviet Union and the liberation of
the countries of Eastern Europe from what Ouspensky called 'the
Plague of Communism'[1] occurred without war, virtually without
violence. During the decades that the world lived with the threat
of nuclear annihilation, such an outcome could not have been
imagined.

The School, The Study Society, Transcendental Meditation,
Gurdjieff groups, and Vedanta study societies, continue to work
and grow around the world. In India the Shankaracharyas continue to provide wisdom to those who seek it. The ancient wisdom

of the East that had long been inaccessible is now available in the Western world.

Some groups are what Ouspensky called 'Fourth Way Schools'. These groups serve several purposes. They provide esoteric knowledge and propitious conditions that make it possible for their members to consciously participate in a process of inner transformation that moves them along a path of spiritual development. Those who work serve as channels for knowledge and subtle energy that uplift the members of the group. Joy Dillingham said one of the aims of a School is to raise the level of the nation. Gurdjieff, Ouspensky, Leon MacLaren, and Dr Roles all believed the Work uplifted humanity.[2] Students' daily interaction with the community provides a positive impulse and allows the influence of a Master Teacher to reach a larger circle of people. One purpose of a Fourth Way School is to make it possible for a rare individual to work toward liberation and achieve full realization, becoming one of the handful of Masters whose power and wisdom channel a harmonizing force that balances the destructive tendencies of the masses and uplifts civilization. These rare few are described in the *Bhagavad Gita*. Shantananda Saraswati said the development of six such men would give birth to a Renaissance – an impulse that would regenerate a civilization.

Dr Scott Gerson was a student in the New York School of Practical Philosophy and a medical doctor who chose to specialize in Ayurvedic medicine. This is an ancient system of medicine practiced for thousands of years in India. The doctor understood the principle enunciated by Gurdjieff that in order for a person to heal the body or attend to the spirit, he must have knowledge of both. He went regularly to India to study this ancient system and its application in unison with today's technology and methods. In India he had an audience with Shantananda Saraswati, who provided guidance and told him to offer meditation to his patients.

---

* Ouspensky's *In Search of the Miraculous,* had originally been titled 'Fragments of an Unknown Teaching' by him.

Dr Gerson established a practice in New York City. Years later, he sought to establish a center for healing and meditation in a contemplative setting outside the city. He asked me to help him find an appropriate property; we looked at several properties, but none were suitable. Six months later he called to tell me he had found and purchased an ideal property. He described the pavilion in Brewster, New York! After confirming details about the property, I informed him that he had purchased the home built by Willem Nyland.

It could be said the bridge built between East and West was begun in the West by Gurdjieff and completed by Shantananda Saraswati through the agency of Dr Roles, Leon MacLaren and Maharishi. Gurdjieff's work, continued by Willem Nyland and others, did not have the benefit of the meditation and only fragments of the Vedanta tradition. But it came to pass that his home, built with his own hands and that of his students, became a center for Meditation and Ayurvedic healing.

In their travels in the early years of the twentieth century, Gurdjieff and Ouspensky had encountered meditation as part of a set of arduous disciplines involving long periods of solitude. It was practiced in seclusion or in a monastic setting. The student spent years practicing physical exercises that prepared him to sit cross-legged, erect, and still for hours. Both men concluded these practices would not be applicable to men and woman in the West. It was in 1947 that Gurudeva in India introduced a modified form of meditation that could be practiced by householders carrying on a full life of family, profession, and community. Gurdjieff and Ouspensky never encountered this form of meditation but their work prepared many students to take up the meditation introduced to the West by Gurudeva's disciple, the Maharishi.

When Dr Roles met the Maharishi, was introduced to the meditation, and the Teaching as expounded by Shantananda Saraswati, he was certain he had found the missing fragments* his first teacher, Ouspensky, had been seeking. The introduction of the meditation to the West by the Maharishi, with the help of

Dr Roles, Leon MacLaren and their students, provided spiritual and emotional nourishment that enriched the lives of individuals and through them provided a harmonizing influence that uplifted society.

The transmission of knowledge from the East to the West is the story of these teachers; the men and women who lived by the principle of 'Learn and teach'. They devoted their lives to the service for truth. They were not perfect, but they strove for perfection. They had failings; they sometimes missed the mark. But their will was strong, and they persevered. As Leon MacLaren said, 'I may have been wrong, but I was never in doubt.' In the stories and memoirs of some of their students there is some criticism of their errors, but as Joy Dillingham said, 'The tree is judged by its finest fruit'. The artist is remembered for his greatest work: by this measure these men and women were truly remarkable, for they provided a conscious impulse for Western Civilization.

In their stories can be seen, for those with eyes to see, the guiding hand of a Universal Intelligence that they all acknowledged and strove to serve with every fiber of their being. These teachers attracted students throughout the twentieth century who tilled the soil in the garden of wisdom.

They worked to realize knowledge in their lives and make it available to others. There were other teachers during the twentieth century whose stories have not been told here; they also lived by the principle of 'Learn and teach', and they also played their roles well. Those who study and Work today stand on a foundation built by many. They are remembered by a few; but more importantly, they remembered themselves. *Their lives and their Work are their heritage.*

A hundred years have passed since Gurdjieff returned to the West to teach. It has been half a century since the introduction of meditation to the West. The teaching of the Eastern masters has been made available in a form accessible and applicable. It has taken root and begun to develop in the minds and hearts of many. The practice of meditation has deepened the spiritual and emotional life of millions. In the East, Western technology has helped to ease the suffering of poverty, and in the early decades of the twenty-first century, we are bearing witness to a communion. It is the unspoken story of the twentieth century, perhaps the greatest story never told:

The Story of *East Meets West*.

The Author

THE AUTHOR had the good fortune to be influenced by some
of the master teachers of the twentieth century. It is useful
to reflect on the influences in one's life that awakened conscience and reason. These profound moments did not just happen,
they were gifts. They were the result of the Work, conscious labors,
love, and sacrifices of others.

Many people during the course of their lives encounter a
teacher, a spiritual path, or a religious experience. Some are interested for a while and then move on to follow other pursuits. Within
some men and women there is a fertile soil for a Teaching or
profound influence to take root and grow. It is embraced by the
heart and mind, nurtured by study and effort and in time matures
to become the aim and purpose of one's life. Gurdjieff called this
fertile soil a Magnetic Center. In *Meetings with Remarkable Men*, he
writes of his father, a man of wisdom and moral strength, who
taught him the discipline to struggle against his own weaknesses;
of a grandmother, who instructed him, 'In life do not do as others
do'; and of a mentor, who instilled in him a love of learning.

A civilization can be uplifted by the conscious labors of a few;
it is sustained by the goodness of many. Ouspensky speaks of the
influences during one's formative years that form in the individual a love of truth and goodness. Engraved in the essence of my
childhood is a memory of 'Goodness', she was my first teacher.

Her name is engraved on a wall on Ellis Island. The building in
New York Harbor is a museum now, but it was the port of entry

for millions of immigrants. Mary was fourteen years old when the ship that transported her across the Atlantic steamed by The Statue of Liberty and delivered its cargo of hopeful pilgrims to America. She was one of the many who left their homeland during the first decade of the twentieth century for the New World. In the small town in Italy where she was born people said, 'In America there is gold in the streets.' She stood with her family on the deck of the ship, their backs to the Old World, as they approached the great city where they would live the rest of their lives.

She was seventeen when she brought home a young man to meet her family. He was tall, upright, handsome, refined and educated, and well-spoken in both Italian and English. He played the violin, the mandolin, and the guitar; he charmed them all. They were married when she was eighteen. He was a good provider who worked for the Long Island Railroad. He worked his way up to the main office where he remained until retirement. He also worked part-time as a musician. That was how they met, at a dance. She approached the band and asked him if they would play a mazurka. Years later when the children asked how they had met he would tease her, 'She flirted with me,' he would say. She was reserved and held herself with dignity and was not pleased by the suggestion that she had been forward. She protested, with the hint of a smile, 'I simply liked the mazurka.' They had five children. I was their first grandson.

He was never unemployed, but during the depression he was one of many who took a cut in pay. She was upset when he told her. He reassured her, 'A smaller paycheck is not a tragedy,' he said. 'No paycheck is a tragedy.' She understood that he was right, but she wanted more for her family; she wanted them to thrive. She was talented and quick with her hands and began to do needlepoint and embroidery at home with great discipline. Occasionally I slept overnight. I don't know what time she awoke, but by nine o'clock she had gone to church, returned home, and finished the housework. One of my earliest memories was of her waking me early.

'Why do I have to get up, Nanna?'

'All of the other rooms are in order,' she said. 'I need to make the bed.' She got me up, made the bed, and made me a special breakfast.

With her husband off to work she took her seat at a peddle-driven sewing machine. Her hands were quick; her attention precise. Her pieces sold for a good price. All traces of her work were put away before her husband came home. Although he knew she was earning extra money, it was never discussed. She would never wish to disrespect him; no one should think this man needed help to support his family.

The extra money helped keep the children well-dressed. They all finished high school, which was uncommon at the time, and the meals were always generous. Her generosity knew no limit, but she wasted nothing. She never failed to turn off the light when she left a room, and she taught me to do the same. When she served me breakfast she cut the napkin in half, saving the other half for lunch. Whenever she could she taught me to help. She would send me to the store and taught me to carefully count the change. She sent me downstairs to the herb garden, to pick basil for the sauce and mint for the lemonade.

Some are gifted with intelligence, some with a pure heart and a strong will, some with a body that has skills and strength. Mary was gifted with all three; she was steady and sure in her movements. I remember her punching a small hole in the corner of a gallon can of olive oil and pouring the oil into serving bottles with openings smaller than a soda bottle. 'Do you want me to get you a funnel, Nanna?' It was not needed, she never spilled a drop. From time to time I have attempted to duplicate the task, but I have never succeeded!

She was a woman of simple faith. They lived in the shadow of a large gothic church that bore her name, 'Mary, Gate of Heaven'. She attended mass daily and had done so for as long as anyone could remember.

On the bureau in her bedroom was a statue of Mary, a rosary, and a candle. In the evening before retiring she would kneel and pray. She prayed for those who had passed on. She prayed for her loved ones. She prayed to express her gratitude, she prayed for strength, and asked for forgiveness. When she heard someone was having difficulties, she did not need to know the details. Her response was the same, she prayed. With all of her being, she wished us well. My aunt told me as I was the first grandson, there was a special place in her heart and prayers for me. Looking back on my life I sense the power and protection of her love and prayers.

For sixty years she had held fast in her Catholicism; daily mass, abstinence from meat on Fridays, days of fasting. Then in the early sixties the Vatican council sought to make the church 'more accessible'. Latin was no longer the language of the Mass. The priest turned to face the people and said the mass in their native language. The ceremony changed and different music was added. The days of fasting and abstinence were no longer required.

'It was one way all of my life,' she said, 'and then everything changed.' The rock her life was built on shifted, but she stood firm. For nearly a billion people the practice of Catholicism changed, but her practice never wavered.

She was a quiet lady. She prayed more than she spoke. No one can ever remember her raising her voice, but when she spoke she always had something to say. When my first child was born I called and told her and she said, 'You are one step higher now.'

She did not attend school in America, but was self-taught and picked up English through usage. She and her husband spoke English in the home, as they did not want the children burdened with an accent. She taught herself to read and write English; her textbooks were the daily newspapers. She spoke with a slight accent and wrote well – the only defect being she spelled phonetically. One day I heard she had won a contest. A recipe she submitted had been selected to appear on the back of a box of pasta. I was impressed. 'Is it a good dish, Nanna?'

'I never made it,' she said.

As a child some of my strongest impressions were the holidays at her home, and the meals she prepared. There were family dinners, and there were also meals she prepared just for me. We lived on the same block, and I visited often. It was just she and I, a grandmother preparing lunch for an eight-year-old boy. I would sit at the kitchen table watching her at the stove, the smell of tomato sauce, seasonings, and something sweet baking in the oven, filled the sunlit room.

'Nanna, your cooking is so good,' I once told her.

She shrugged, 'Fifty years,' she said.

'No Nanna, it's really good! Nanna, when I grow up I am going to bring my wife to dinner. I want her to cook like you.' She did not look up from the stove, but I saw her smile, and she put a little something extra into that lunch. It was a blessing that she lived to be eighty-four. My wife knew her well, learned many of her recipes, and a child's simple wish came true.

When I heard she was dying I called my aunt and said I wanted to see her. She was in a hospital, and my aunt said, 'It is not pretty, John.' When I arrived at the hospital, I found her delirious. Her eyes were closed. She spoke but made no sense. I stood by her bed and held her hand, squeezing it from time to time, but there was no response. My aunt and I spoke quietly. Nanna was not with us. I squeezed her hand again. She stopped speaking; she opened her eyes and saw me. The pained expression on her face fell away.

She said, 'Take Care of Your Self, Johnny.'

And then she fell asleep. Her last words to me were in the same spirit as all the others I remember. *She wished me well.*

My cousin David was her youngest grandson. He lived nearby and once a week his mother brought him over for the afternoon while she did some errands. David also marveled at her meals. When he graduated high school he knew what he wanted to do. He went to the Culinary Arts Institute. It was there that he grew to appreciate what had gone into those meals: the shopping, the preparation, and the seasonings; dishes that held generations

Mary Chiddo
This photo was taken in 1912 on her wedding day.
She was eighteen years old.

of tradition. After graduation he started working in New York and then in California. He met some businessmen who took him to Japan where American cuisine was growing in popularity. David became a well-known chef in Japan, and had a cooking program on Japanese television. Once during a televised interview he was asked about the photograph that hung on the wall behind him.

'It's my grandmother,' he said. 'The meals she prepared for me when I was a child inspired my career.'

She showered us all with love, she nurtured our souls.

The study of philosophy and this journey of Self-discovery began in 1967. A few years out of college, there was often a feeling of being vaguely uneasy. There was little sense of purpose; my job provided little satisfaction, a girl I had been seeing had just ended the relationship. A desire began to stir for a deeper understanding of myself, a deeper insight about life. But I had no idea what I was looking for or where to look.

I was with a group of friends one Saturday afternoon where two of the women were having a serious conversation to which I was barely listening. One of them exclaimed, 'You have read Ouspensky?!' 'Yes,' said the other, '*In Search of the Miraculous.*' They were so enthusiastic I asked about the book and wrote down the title and author. A year later I found out that the mother of one of the women had met Ouspensky and had been in one of his groups before her daughter or I were born.

The next weekend I visited three book stores without success. Before the internet finding a book, a group, or anything could be difficult. I thought this might be important so I continued to look. Someone referred me to Weiser's Book Store that had a section on Eastern Philosophy. At last I found the book along with others by Ouspensky, Gurdjieff, and their students.

Ouspensky had my attention from the first page. Writing about the obvious contradictions of daily life, the daydreams, circling thoughts, random associations and fleeting attention span, he described our ordinary mental condition as a 'waking sleep'. He said it was possible for men and women to 'wake up', but one needed knowledge not generally available, an effort he called 'Work', and the help of a group or school with a common aim.

His descriptions of our state of mind were irrefutable: many things were verified by experience and observation. After a few chapters I stopped to consider how, being well read and college educated, I had never heard of this writer or his philosophy. I finished the book, made frequent trips to Weiser's for other books and began to look for a 'group'.

One evening a friend brought over an older man, it seemed he was my friend's mentor. A few of us were engaged in animated conversation. I was doing a lot of the talking when I remembered something Ouspensky had written. He had described a meeting where new people came and were so full of themselves, they did all the talking and left having heard nothing. I stopped speaking, asked the man a question and let him lead the conversation. He had a great deal of life experience, and the evening was well spent. At the end of this encounter I realized something had changed – *I was ready to listen.*

One afternoon I left Weiser's bookstore and got on a subway with a book by Ouspensky that I had just purchased. *The Psychology of Man's Possible Evolution* was a collection of his lectures that had just been published. I was standing up in the train reading the book when I was tapped on the shoulder. A man held up a copy of the same book. He asked over the roar of the train, 'Are you interested in these ideas?'

I leaned closer to him so I could be heard and answered: 'Yes, and I am looking for a group.'

He said he was on his way to meet a friend, and I was welcome to join him. I had plans for the evening but decided they were not as important. So, I rode with him to Brooklyn.

He took me to an apartment where he introduced me to

Douglas Oberwager. 'This is John; he has an interest in the Work.' Douglas, a man with steel blue eyes and a firm handshake, was older than I, but his youthful appearance and energy were misleading. I did not realize until many years later that he was over twenty years older. As he shook my hand, he looked me directly in the eye and asked: 'What do you want?'

'Knowledge,' I answered.

'That is too general. Knowledge is a means. Some men want money, some power, some recognition. Practically speaking, what do you want?'

'Well,' I hesitated, 'I would like to improve my relationships with women,' not sure if that was an appropriate answer.

'That is something that can be worked with,' he said. 'To have that kind of improvement you need to be more of a man and there is much in this Work about that. That is an aim, something you are willing to work for, and now that I know your aim I can relate to you intelligently. You are seeking knowledge about yourself, and that begins with observation, self-observation, and self-examination.'

So began my relationship with Douglas. We would meet about once every two weeks and usually had a telephone conversation in between. The relationship was unique. Answering the phone I was greeted by 'Can you wake up? Now!' The conversation never wandered off subject. We spoke about what had been observed, what had been read since our last meeting. These were not theoretical discussions. The aim was always to be present – not drift off into random associations – to raise the level of awareness, not generally, but now! We spent long evenings together, sometimes with others who shared our interest, though rarely our intensity. We would meet in my apartment or visit friends. We would go to cafes or places where we could mingle with others, but always with the same aim, to experience a refined state of attention, to observe oneself and include everything around us. Whoever we encountered, Douglas would draw into his orbit, they would become part of the experience, and even the waiter or cab driver would be drawn in. One waiter began to meet with us regularly.

One evening after we had been meeting for over a year I said: 'Wait a minute Douglas, who are you? I don't know anything about you. Do you have a family? How do you earn a living?'

'Oh, you want to be subjective, all right, but that is not the basis of our relationship. My father passed on, I see my mother regularly, I have a sister who is married with a child. I was married once. It didn't work out, but we are friends.'

He continued, 'My father had an auto dealership. From the time I got out of college I worked with him. We sold a lot of cars, made a lot of money. When he died the family sold the business and I bought an annuity. I live modestly, it is more than enough. I like to sail, I have done some photography, but I only have one interest now and that is this Work. Now that is enough of that, we were talking about balance between mind, heart, and body, and we have drifted into the past, now can we bring the body into view, can you feel the weight of the body...'

After two years of making inquiries and visiting two groups, I learned the time and place of a meeting being led by Willem Nyland. I did not have an invitation but decided to attend. When I walked in, a receptionist asked my name and who had invited me. To my surprise, Douglas was near the door and vouched for me. The meeting was being held in a ground floor apartment on the upper west side of Manhattan. As I entered the room, Nyland was sitting at the front of the room. Next to him sat a man with a tape recorder. The rows of chairs were all occupied, and people were standing tightly packed in the aisle. I stood about twenty feet from him. He was a thin man in his late seventies with grey hair and eyes that held you in a penetrating gaze; he spoke for forty-five minutes without notes, then the tape was turned over and he answered questions. To keep the street noise from being recorded the windows were closed. The temperature in the crowded room became uncomfortable, but no one left.

Nyland spoke with authority and clarity. He spoke quietly but with a force and power that affected everyone in the room. He talked about Gurdjieff and this Work, as well as the need for men and woman to strive for something more than the ordinary pursuits of life. He explained the method of impartial observation and how it could be applied during the activities of daily life. When questions were asked it was apparent that the questioners were serious about this inquiry. They had read Gurdjieff and Ouspensky and had attempted to apply this method of observation. They asked questions based on their efforts 'to wake up', and reported on the results of these efforts and the difficulties they encountered. They had not come to hear a lecture or merely out of curiosity; they had some experience with this Work and wanted to incorporate it into their lives. I had found a 'group'. They came and sat or stood in this hot room because this man was speaking from a level of awareness above and beyond the ordinary. Nyland had been with Gurdjieff for twenty-five years and had lived and taught this Work for twenty more. I had found a fixed star upon which to set my course.

After the meeting I asked Douglas why he had not led me to the group. He replied, 'The first test for membership of a group is to find the door, the work here requires serious effort. If you didn't have the persistence and wherewithal to find the group, you wouldn't get very far.' The answer was not easy to accept, but it was in keeping with the methods of Gurdjieff and Ouspensky, who never made it easy for the seeker. In fact as the conditions in the overcrowded room demonstrated, they sometimes made it difficult.

Douglas and I attended Nyland's group for the next five years. Douglas was my first teacher, and he became my closest friend. When I married, he was my best man. With marriage and then children our meetings grew less frequent and of shorter duration.

There were times when months would pass between contacts, but the relationship remained constant.

I called him one evening to read him something I had found. He was in bed with the flu so our conversation was shorter than usual. He said he had met a Sufi and had found some of the teachers of Gurdjieff. His energy was low so I suggested he rest. A few days later I received a call from the head of a Sufi Order; Douglas had died. He had heard we were close friends, and he invited me to a memorial service.

Later a group of about thirty people – friends, family, and neighbors, gathered in a circle, each spoke about Douglas. Their relationship was not our relationship, but many spoke of what they had learned from him; it seemed he never stopped teaching. We had worked together for twenty years.

About forty days after his passing, it became apparent something had shifted. Impediments that I had struggled with for years dissolved. At times I experienced a clarity that had not been available before. Douglas once told me that when a man of substance passes on he sometimes takes with him a veil of illusion, an impediment that had inhibited the development of someone close to him. It was a remarkable gift from a remarkable friend. As I reflect on our twenty-year friendship, from our first conversation in his apartment to our final phone call, I do not believe we ever had a meaningless conversation. I could not say that Douglas always remembered himself, but he was a man who never forgot his aim.

Shortly after Nyland's death in 1975, I returned to the New York School of Practical Philosophy where I had the good fortune to come under the guidance of Joy Dillingham and Leon MacLaren, and the guiding light of Shantanda Saraswati.

The journey toward Truth and Self-discovery is made possible by the remarkable men and women who devoted their lives to this Work. Their stories are our heritage and a source of inspiration, their example a course of instruction. The author's aim is to record this heritage that it may be remembered and inspire others.

The journey continues; I have engaged in this Work with men and women from New York, Boston, Canada, England, Ireland, Amsterdam, Italy, Australia, and other countries. We share a common aim: to remember One Self. Our lives intertwine; they form part of an infinite pattern woven in eternity. It has been a privilege to travel with them on this 'Voyage of Discovery'.

John Adago lives with his wife in New York City. He is available to speak to groups and can be reached at johnadago@gmail.com. Visit: thejourneyback.net for more quotes and stories.

Meditation

Appendix 1

Words of the Wise

THIS COLLECTION of quotes reflects the wisdom and philosophy of the teachers whose stories have been told.

One needs to Work along three lines:

The first is Work on oneself, to remember one Self.

The second line is Work for and with others, to acknowledge the Self in others.

The third line is Work for the sake of the Work. OUSPENSKY

It is only the body which is born and then dissolved; the dweller neither comes from anywhere nor goes anywhere. So the preparation for death is to establish complete detachment from the body. When the mortal body dissolves back to the physical elements, the soul remains until the next time around. It will only be dissolved at full liberation.

Therefore, in truth, not much importance needs to be given to the death of the physical body. Our efforts should be directed at preparing for total liberation. To achieve that one has to be alert and awake, so that the soul can be purified through knowledge and meditation.

SHANTANANDA SARASWATI

The ordinary man is not free in his manifestations, in his life, or in his moods. He cannot be what he would like to be; and what he considers himself to be, he is not. At the same time, man should indeed be the acme of creation, since he is formed with and has in himself all the possibilities for acquiring all the data exactly similar to the data existing in He Who Actualizes Everything Existing in the Universe.

GURDJIEFF

When you demand nothing of the world, nor of God, when you want nothing, seek nothing, expect nothing; then the Supreme state will come to you uninvited and unexpected.

SHRI NIJARGATTA MAHARAJ

To be still and listen without judgment is to Self-remember.

DR ROLES

A prayer is a wish made in mind, heart, and body combined with an effort made in mind, heart, and body.

GURDJIEFF

The Good is one, the pleasant another; both command the soul.

KATHA UPANISHAD

Blessed is he who does his work as well as he can, for from such work perfection arises.

BHAGAVAD GITA

Ours is the right to the work, not to the fruit thereof.
Let not your motive be the fruit of your action

BHAGAVAD GITA

We do not work for results but that does not mean there are no results. If there are no results, then you are not working correctly.

WILLEM NYLAND

An aversion or attachment to anything is a clue that there is Work to be done.

RAM DASS

We do not do, but without us nothing is done...

The question is not what to do, but how to see...

I need to realize that the act of seeing brings something entirely new, a new possibility of vision, certainty, and knowledge...

So long as I have not seen the nature and movement of the mind, there is little sense in believing I could be free of it...

JEANE DE SALZMANN

One hears of the Spirit with surprise, another thinks it marvelous, the third listens without comprehending. Thus, though many are told about it, scarcely is there one who knows it.

BHAGAVAD GITA

The natures of men and women are distinct. Men require knowledge, a fixed star on which to set their course, and the encouragement to complete the journey. Women need only be reminded of what they already understand. Their role is to *care for the creation*. Women come into the creation carrying little bundles of doubt. They need praise, appreciation, affirmation, and to love and be loved.

JOY DILLINGHAM

Faith and fear cannot live under one roof, choose faith.

KEN JACOBS

Go the whole hog, including the postage.

GURDJIEFF

Before you begin anything, you have first to do something else.

ANGELO KEITH

The role of the entrepreneur is to make the system work.

NEIL BROXMEYER
former leader of the New York
School of Practical Philosophy

You can have anything you want, but you have to take everything that comes along with it.

JOY DILLINGHAM

The 'to do list' never ends.

BARRY STEINGARD
leader of the New York School
of Practical Philosophy

You can't make a good deal with a bad person.   WARREN BUFFET

Remember, dear, you don't have to judge 'The Ideas' by the people who believe in them.

JESSMIN HOWARTH

He who sees the Self in all others, all others in One Self, knows no sorrow.

ISHA UPANISHAD

The *point* of it all… is the *point* of it all.   MR WHITING
leader of The London
School of Meditation

Ultimately, knowledge in action is all that matters.

SHANTANANDA SARASWATI

God made sense turn outward… Now and again a daring man… looked back and found Himself.

KATHA UPANISHAD

Speaking to a group of teenagers about meditation, he asked, 'Do you love your parents?'
    They answered, 'Yes.'

'Do you want to be just like them?'
They answered more emphatically, 'No!'
'Well, if you don't meditate, you will.'

SHANE MULHALL
leader of the School of
Philosophy in Ireland

Anything done for another is done for oneself.   POPE JOHN PAUL II

To man it is given, to have what he wishes, and be what he wants.

POPE INNOCENT III

Art, in its highest form, is an attempt to express the inexpressible.

JOY DILLINGHAM

During a lecture Joy Dillingham was asked, 'Does the School have a position on evil?'
    She answered, 'We don't like it.'

Luke smiled impatiently, 'I have discovered that philosophers always have a story. Life is short. Why is it that scholars treat time as if it did not exist and there is an eternity for discussion?'
    'For the reason,' said the scholar, 'that time does not exist and there is an eternity for discussion.'

TAYLOR CALDWELL
Dear and Glorious Physician

Quantum theory reveals a basic oneness of the universe. It shows that we cannot decompose the world into independently existing small units. As we penetrate into matter, nature does not show us any isolated 'basic building blocks,' but rather appears as a complicated web of relations between various parts of the whole. These relations always include the observer in an essential way.

FRITJOF CAPRA
The Tao of Physics

The whole is present in each part, in each level of existence. The living reality, which is unbroken and undivided, is in everything.

DAVID BOHM
physicist

In order to go anywhere one must have a fixed point of reference, an aim; then you can know your left from your right. In life men think they are moving somewhere, but this is illusion. For all their activity, they move no more than a squirrel in a wheel. When the impressions octave does not develop, the machine functions as a pig or a sheep fattened for the slaughter.

Nature provides for him some enjoyment, for without enjoyment no man can live. But wherever there is pleasure, there will also be pain. By rushing after the one, a man must suffer the other.

What is the first characteristic of self-remembering? In this state man is not centre. He is not separate. Sitting in a room, he is aware of the whole room, of himself as only one of the objects in it. He is likewise aware of others and does not put himself above them or criticize or judge. This is not love, but it is the beginning of love. In this state a man has no self as he is usually aware of it. It is quite impossible for him to consider or become negative, for the moment he does so the state will vanish.

MADAME SOPHIE OUSPENSKY

The job of philosophy begins with visualization of the Absolute, and ends with becoming the Absolute.

SITARAM JAISWAL

Movement from movement is agitation, movement from stillness is creation. One learns to be happy without being excited and disappointed without being agitated.

SITARAM JAISWAL

When true knowledge becomes your own, then it can be called wisdom. Realization is instantaneous, and takes place when ignorance is dissolved. The way to unity is through meditation, true knowledge, love, and devotion.

SHANTANANDA SARASWATI

In the world of causes everything must be consciousness, because it is in itself consciousness. Consciousness is the soul of the world.

The mystery of time permeates everything...

The mystery of thought creates everything...

The mystery of infinity is the greatest of all mysteries...

OUSPENSKY
Terium Organum

Is there any part of life where you will fare worse by attending and better by not? To-day I choose to play. Play with attention? I choose to sing. What prevents you from singing with attention? Does the captain of a ship manage it better by not attending? Are any of the smaller acts of life done better by inattention? If the procrastination of attention is profitable, the complete omission is more profitable; but if it is not profitable, why don't you maintain your attention constantly?

When you let your attention go even for a short time, do not imagine you will recover it when you choose; but keep in mind that in consequence of the fault committed to-day your affairs must be in a worse condition for all that follows.

For first, you form a habit of not attending; then a habit of deferring attention. And by deferring it, you drive away from your life happiness, proper behavior, and harmonious living.

EPICTETUS

I must confess, before encountering this Work, I never thought of life as a thing to think of.

DR MAURICE NICOLL

The unexamined life is not worth living.

SOCRATES

We should never accommodate a doubt. Even if we have only one moment to live, we should forsake all worry about the past or the future and make good use of the present, in a manner worthy of the dignity of the Atman.

SHANTANANDA SARASWATI

Two things must be cut short; fear of the future and memory of past discomfort; the one does not concern us anymore; the other does not concern us yet.

Be liberated from these worries that torture the mind; be happy with the present moment and know that you need not be content with very little, for you will have everything.

EPICTETUS

One man stands firm on a shaky place, another stands uncertain on a firm place. A wise man would pause before saying who was in the better position.

JOY DILLINGHAM

A deep meaning and many subtle allegories appeared in what only yesterday had seemed to be naive popular fantasy or crude super-stition. And the greatest mystery and the greatest miracle was that the thought became possible that death may not exist, that those who have gone may not have vanished altogether, but exist some-where and somehow, and that perhaps I may see them again. I have become so accustomed to think 'scientifically' that I am afraid even to imagine that there may be something else beyond the outer covering of life. I feel like a man condemned to death, whose companions have been hanged, and who has already become reconciled to the thought that the same fate awaits him; and suddenly he hears that his companions are alive, that they have escaped and that there is hope also for him. And he fears to believe this, because it would be so terrible if it proved to be false, and nothing would remain but prison and the expectation of execution.

OUSPENSKY
A New Model of the Universe

A man can be given only what he can use; and he can use only that for which he has sacrificed something.

OUSPENSKY
The Strange Life of Ivan Osokin

It is impossible to learn what you already think you know.

EPICTETUS

Constantly remind yourself, I am a member of the whole body of conscious things. If you think of yourself as a mere part, then love for mankind will not well up in your heart; you will look for some reward in every act of kindness and miss the boon which the act itself is offering. Then all your work will be seen as a mere duty and not as the very portal connecting you with the Universe itself.

MARCUS AURELIUS

Withdraw and look within. If you do not see your own beauty, do as the sculptor does; he removes one part, scrapes another, makes one area smooth, and cleans the other, until the beautiful face appears in the statue.

In the same way, you must remove everything that is superfluous, straighten that which is crooked, and purify all that is dark until you make it brilliant with beauty.

Never cease chiseling your statue until the godlike splendor of virtue shines out from it, until you see perfect goodness surely established in the stainless shrine.

PLOTINUS

We are already one. But we imagine we are not. What we have to recover is our original unity. What we have to be is what we are.

THOMAS MERTON

Your 'sentences', will be your sentences.

JOY DILLINGHAM

Truth is One, Paths are many.

Selflessness is the key to Spiritual life.   SWAMI SATCHIDANANDA

We seek the truth as if it were a distant aim. Working to get nearer to it, and see it clearer and clearer.

WILLEM NYLAND

Let nothing come between you and the Light.

HENRY DAVID THOREAU

That ye, being rooted and grounded in love, may be able to comprehend with all the saints; what is the breadth, the length, the depth, and the height …

THE APOSTLE PAUL
Letter to the Ephesians 1:11, 17-18

We need to find God, and He cannot be found in noise and restlessness. God is the friend of silence. See how nature − trees, flowers, grass, grow in silence; see the stars, moon, and the sun, how they move in silence … We need silence to be able to touch souls.

MOTHER TERESA

Be still and know that I am God.   PSALM 46:10

The product of Truth is Faith.
The product of Faith is Love.
The product of Love is Service.

MOTHER TERESA

It is not a dogma that I leave you, but the capacity to find truth in itself and for itself.

BUDDHA

Truth alone triumphs, not untruth. Stand upon Truth and you have got God.

VIVEKANANDA

The Truth shall set you free. JESUS

Meditation and spiritual disciplines are not practiced for personal gain; the man in a church tower does not ring the bell for himself. May it be remembered that what is known and what is written arises from a Universal Force that gives movement to all things.

AUTHOR'S PRAYER

Appendix 2

The Enneagram

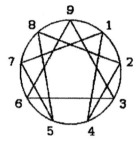

THE ENNEAGRAM is a symbol that embodies three universal laws. A circle is divided into nine points. The **Law of Seven** is represented in the Enneagram by dividing 1 by 7 which yields a progression: 1428571... These points are connected on the circle depicting the Law of Seven. The numbers 3, 6, and 9 are connected to form a triangle depicting The Law of Three.

The circle symbolizes the **Law of One**, all encompassing, without beginning or end. One is the beginning of all numbers, and there is no number that is not based upon one. In the Vedanta Philosophy, Advaita, literally means, not two. As Adi Shankara wrote in *The Brahma Sutra*, the entire creation is held in Consciousness. Consciousness is the causal principle of all and everything. The one all-pervading Consciousness is also the sustaining principle of every form and manifestation. As all forms and manifestations change, Consciousness is the one unchanging constant. When Consciousness is withdrawn, the form or manifestation ceases to exist. In Vedanta this all pervading creative principle is called Brahman. This Consciousness is the same Consciousness that is, in fact, One Self; what Vedanta calls Atman; what Judaism and Christianity call the Soul; what Gurdjieff and Ouspensky called 'I'. *The Chhandogya Upanishad* says, 'Ayam Atma Brahma'. This Atman Is Brahman. Or as Moses said, 'I Am that I Am'.

The **Law of Seven** can be seen in a ray of light fragmenting into the seven colors of the spectrum. Astronomers/astrologers based their observations on the seven bodies that could be seen with the naked eye. Their names became the basis of the seven-day week and the calendar. The law can be heard in the seven notes of the octave. It is the Law that governs creation and the law that governs the way back to the Source of all and everything.

An impulse enters at Do. Re and Mi will follow, but in order to cross the next interval at Fa, another impulse must enter or that which began with Do will stop or alter direction. This is called 'the Fa Bridge'. The momentum from the impulse will carry through So, La, and Si, but another impulse must enter at the Si-Do interval.

We see this in our everyday affairs. At Do, the beginning of any endeavor, an effort must be made. Having begun, momentum will carry on for the next two steps, Re and Mi. However, we then encounter an obstacle, the Fa bridge. If an effort is not made the endeavor will stop or alter direction. Having made the second effort, momentum will carry through steps So, La, Si. As we know from experience many an endeavor is not completed because of the lack of effort needed to bring the project to completion. So an impulse is needed at the Si-Do interval to complete the octave.

For one on a Way seeking liberation at these intervals, a Conscious Impulse must enter or the mechanical laws of nature will alter the aspirant's course. This impulse must come from a teacher or interaction with a group or a School. In time the aspirant learns to cross the interval by Remembering Himself.

The **Law of Three** states that a phenomenon or manifestation is the result of the confluence of three forces. This is seen in natural law as the active, passive and neutral or reconciling force. It is given expression in many traditions. Confucius speaks of yin, yang, and the Tao. Vedanta speaks of the three gunas: rajas, tamas, and sattva.

Christianity speaks of The Trinity: the Father, Son and Holy Spirit, three aspects of the omnipresent Divinity

Gurdjieff introduced the symbol of The Enneagram to the West to elucidate these universal laws.

Appendix 3

Philosophy and Christianity

Although you study Indian philosophy, you are not Hindu. You were born into a Judeo-Christian tradition. The religion of your birth is a gift from the Absolute. There is great value in these traditions. You would be wise to practice your religion.

Sitaram Jaiswal, speaking in New York, 1998

A CHILD RAISED in the Christian tradition hears stories from the Gospels. Simple stories about talents and seeds, fishermen and shepherds, masters and servants; the parables nurture conscience. They instill a belief in goodness and virtue in the mind and heart of the child. Later, the study of philosophy may illuminate many of these stories and reveal a deeper meaning.

Paul was the first disciple to bring the teachings of Christ to those outside the Jewish community. He was a fierce persecutor of the early Christians until he had a revelation on, 'the road to Damascus' (Acts 9:1-19, Acts 26:12-18). He became a fearless advocate who laid the foundation of the early church. The breadth of his travels is impressive even to modern man; he brought the Judeo-Christian tradition to the Greeks and Romans, and others. His letters to those ancient churches continue to instruct and inspire two thousand years later.

In a letter to the Corinthians (I Cor. 12:6), Paul wrote:

> There are diversities of gifts, but the same Spirit. And there are diversities of operations, but it is the same God which worketh all in all. For to one is given by the Spirit, the word of wisdom, to another knowledge ... to another faith ... to another the gift of healing. But all these worketh that one and the *selfsame Spirit*... Whether we be Jews or Gentiles, bond or free ... For the body is, and hath many members, and all the members of that one body, being many, are one body.

The Work described in this book attracts people from all walks of life: men and women, young and old, professionals and tradesmen, students and scholars. But Paul would remind us we are all members of one body, all of the 'selfsame Spirit'. Paul would call us all catholic. The word means universal, all-inclusive, from universe, one verse, one song, one body of principles. Those who are drawn to this Work share a common interest. We seek to know the truth. We seek a deeper understanding of the meaning of our lives, and the answers to fundamental questions. What am I? What are the laws that govern the creation? What is my relationship to the creation and the Creator? In every age master teachers have provided answers to these fundamental questions. We find the truth in the East and the West, in the Old and New Testament, in the Upanishads, and the writings of Socrates, Hermes Trismegistus, and others. In the philosophical material presented at the School of Practical Philosophy, one hears quotes from many sources, both eastern and western. For the pursuit of truth reveals there is a unifying chord that sounds through all the great teachings. By way of analogy, if we were to enter a room and find there gathered Jesus, Moses, Shankara, Buddha, Socrates, Hermes, and Krishna, I do not believe we would find them engaged in an argument. What the master teachers understood and taught was universal and unchanging – they taught the Truth. Virtually all spiritual traditions and philosophical systems acknowledge a power that created the universe and sustains life. And that this power manifests as universal principles that transcend time, place, and culture. The forms of their teachings are adapted to meet the conditions of time and place, but the principles they taught are universal.

As Shantananda Saraswati expressed it:

> Human beings everywhere are the same and so they have common desires and aspirations. One of the most universal of these aspirations is happiness. All religions everywhere have as their aim the achievement of happiness or bliss. Differences in religions are not found in their aim but in there rituals. These rituals have different forms and characters according to the geographical place and time of their origin. If one looks behind these rituals, one can see the fundamental spiritual activities of man are practically the same everywhere.*

If philosophy were to be summed up in one word that word would be 'unity'. In the Vedanta philosophy the Sanskrit word *advaita* means 'not two' (*dvaita* means 'two').

Jesus gave expression to this unity in Mark 12:29-31:

> Hear O Israel; The Lord our God is one Lord: and thou shalt love the Lord thy God with all thy heart, and with all thy soul, and with all thy mind, and with all thy strength: this is the first commandment. And the second is… Thou shalt love thy neighbor as thyself.

Religion speaks of one God, philosophy speaks of an unchanging Truth. But in our ordinary state we do not acknowledge unity. We view the world from duality. The perspective is me and the rest of the creation. And we act as if we were the center of the creation. Every impression is colored by our consideration of how this will affect my well-being and satisfy my desires. And so upon hearing a weather report, our association is our weekend plans, for example, and how the weather might affect those plans. And perhaps we make a silent prayer that atmospheric conditions might shift so as not to interfere with our pleasure. The message

* Conversation with Dr Roles preserved by The Study Society.

of the master teachers was designed to liberate us from the illusion of duality, from this egocentric view so that we might realize the Unity of One God, One Truth, One Self.

John the Baptist was 'the voice of one crying out in the wilderness' (Mark 1:3). Those wandering in the wilderness are the masses without the benefit of the Truth. He called on mankind to wake up from the egocentric view, of our ordinary state: as Jesus said (Mark 8:18), 'Having eyes, see ye not? And having ears, hear ye not?' John called on mankind 'to repent'. Repent is derived from the Latin word *penitire,* to think (translated from the Greek word *metanoia*). To repent is to rethink or to have a change of mind. He was urging mankind to rise above the illusion of duality and acknowledge One God, One Truth, One Spirit. He called on them to prepare for the coming of a Messiah, a savior, a teacher who would liberate mankind from the bondage of duality and the illusion of our egocentric perspective, to remind us that 'we are all of the selfsame Spirit'.

What is a Messiah?

Leon MacLaren spoke of the hierarchy of man, of seven levels of development. The highest level was one who had achieved a state of the permanent realization of Unity. He lives in a constant state of Remembering One Self. He has gone through the process of inner transformation:

1 Learning the truth.
2 Living the truth.
3 Becoming the living truth.

Jesus was man number eight. He was not born to learn the truth, He was born to show mankind the Way. As it is expressed in the Gospel of John (1:14), 'the Word was made flesh, and dwelt among us ... full of grace and truth'.

As a child matures he begins to describe himself as a man, a student, an American, a Christian. And each qualifier imposes a limit on the universal Self. Jesus did not describe Himself as a carpenter, a Nazarene, a teacher, or a Jew. In his own words, He said:

'I am the way, the truth, and the life.' (John 14:6)

'I am the light of the world.' (John 8:12; 9:5)

'I and my Father are One.' (John 10:30)

'Ye shall know that I am in my Father, and ye are in me, and I am in you.' (John 14:20)

'I say unto you, before Abraham was, I am.' (John 8:58)

He was not born bound by ideas of culture, time, place, or the illusion of duality. He was born pure, perfect, and complete. He was born free of 'original sin.' These are the symbolic meanings of the virgin birth.

The life of Christ is a living teaching. All the events taking place on a physical level also have a symbolic meaning. The entire story is a parable with ever deeper levels of meaning to discover as reason and understanding awaken.

Jesus did not write down his teaching, He lived it. His words and deeds have passed down through the generations. His teaching has been engraved in the minds and hearts of mankind. He taught through parables, stories laden with levels of meaning that are revealed to the disciple according to his level of understanding. One of the first parables He spoke was the story of a man sowing seeds (Matthew 13:2-9):

> And great multitudes were gathered together unto him, so that he went into a ship and sat: and the whole multitude stood on the shore and he spoke many things to them in parables saying, Behold, a sower went forth to sow; and when he sowed, some seeds fell by the way side and fowls came and devoured them up. Some fell upon stony places where there was no depth of earth … and because they had no root they withered away. And some fell among thorns, and the thorns sprung up and choked them; and some fell on good earth and grew and brought forth fruit, some a hundredfold, some sixtyfold and some thirtyfold. Who hath ears to hear, let him hear.

Later when he was alone with his disciples He said (Matthew 13:11; Mark 4:11; Luke 8:10), 'It is given to you to know the mysteries, but to them it is not given and so I speak to them in parables.' Then He explained that He is the sower, the seeds are his teaching, and the soil is the minds and hearts of men.

Jesus said of this parable (Mark 4:13), 'Know ye not this parable? And how then will ye know all parables?'

Also, consider the setting; the people are standing on the shore, their feet are on the earth, their perspective is the material world. Jesus is in a boat on the water. Water represents the spiritual world. His perspective is the world of spirit. He is with them but He is not of them. Here He is teaching how to read the parables and the Gospels, for all the stories have both a literal and a symbolic meaning.

The study of philosophy is the way of reason. Christ taught the way of love. Love and reason are like the two wings of the dove; both are needed to transcend the material world. Some of the parables appear in more than one gospel. The parable of the fishes and loaves appears in all four Gospels. It's told a total of seven times (Matthew 14:17; 15:34; 16:9; Mark 6:38; 8:5; Luke 9:13; John 6:9). It is a parable about the power of love.

Jesus departed out of the city and a large crowd followed to hear him teach. And when evening came and time to depart, Jesus said (Matthew 15:32), 'I have compassion on the multitude.' He said, 'They cannot travel home without nourishment for many will fall faint.' But his disciples replied (Matthew 15:34), 'But we have but seven loaves and a few fishes.' And Jesus took the loaves and fishes, and looking up to heaven, He blessed them and gave them to His disciples to give to the people. After they had eaten, the remnants were gathered and they filled twelve baskets. And those who had eaten were more than five thousand.

'He hath compassion on the multitude.' It is love that performs the miracle. The fishes and loaves, like the seeds, are His teaching. 'For man cannot live by bread alone but by every word from the mouth of God' (Matthew 4:4; Luke 4:4). The blessing, the teaching, originates with Christ, but it is passed on by the disciples; for it is through men and women living according to the example of Christ that divine love manifests among mankind.

The multiplication of the loaves and fishes allows all to receive what they need, for what appeared to be want was revealed to be abundance. The 'multiplication' is the manifestation of love in the lives of men and women. This is the power of love, what appears to be want is revealed to be universal abundance.

At the last supper he taught the culmination of his teaching. He said, 'This is my commandment, That ye love one another, as I have loved you' (John 15:12).

In the story of the prodigal son (Luke 15:11-32) we are taught some fundamental principles. The son goes to his father and asks, 'for that portion of goods that falleth unto him'. He is asking for his inheritance.

The Prodigal son is the younger son. Here youth refers not to age, but lack of wisdom. He leaves the love and protection of his Father and goes to a far-off land, 'to spend his substance in outrageous living'. He pursues the satisfaction of his desires, which lead him to want and deprivation. He sinks to the level of the pigsty. The pigs symbolize the coarsest of desires. The want and pain wake him up, he remembers that he is his Father's son. He remembers 'himself' and turns toward his Father and begins the journey home. In the Katha Upanishad it says, 'The good is one, the pleasant another; both command the soul.' Choosing the satisfaction of his desires led him to depravity. Choosing the good led him on to the path back to his Father.

He doesn't have to go far: his Father meets him along the way. This is the law. Once one turns toward the truth, the first steps toward home are illuminated and one is given the strength to take those steps. And he is welcomed back into the love and protection of his Father's home. Jesus expressed this law, 'Ask, and it shall be given; seek, and ye shall find; knock, and it shall be opened unto you' (Matthew 7:7; Luke 11:9).

The second son is standing outside his Father's house. He does not join the celebration. He is resentful of the welcome his brother has received, he is slighted that his loyalty and service are not being acknowledged. The prodigal son was cut off from his

Father's love by greed and lust; the older brother has cut himself off through resentment, anger, and jealousy – what are called the negative emotions. Leon MacLaren wrote, 'The expression of negative emotions gives rise to endless pain and suffering.' Jesus said (Matthew 15:11), 'Not that which goes into the mouth that defileth a man, but that which cometh out of the mouth, this defileth a man.' The older brother argues that he has obeyed him 'these many years'. The Father answers with wisdom and mercy, 'And he said unto him, son, thou art ever with me, and all that I have is thine. It was meet that we should make merry, and be glad; for this thy brother was dead, and is alive again: and was lost and is found' (Luke 15:31,32).

And who are we? The prodigal son who awakens from shame and despair and returns to the source of all good? Are we the obedient, but resentful son, unable to rejoice in his brother's salvation? Or are we the merciful and forgiving Father, who views his sons with love and wisdom? We can see in ourselves both brothers, and with grace we may exemplify the Father.

Then there is the question of the inheritance, that which he was entitled to by birth. What is being spoken about is what we have been given. The circumstances and talents we inherit. What of this inheritance? When he remembers that he is his Father's son he says, 'Make of me as one of your servants.' For he knows the wages are good in the vineyard of the Lord. He remembers that his role is to serve. It is for this purpose that he has been given his strengths and talents.

What to do with what has been given is further illuminated in the parable of the master who is going on a journey (Matthew 25: 14-30). He summons three servants and gives into their care talents, one five, one two, one a single one, each according to his ability. When the master returns he summons his servants. The first used the talents in trade, and he returned ten talents to the master. The second did likewise and returned four talents, and the master was pleased. He bestowed cities unto their care, for they had shown ability in caring for small things and so were given greater responsibility. The third servant had buried the talent, and he returned the one talent. The master was not pleased, and the servant was cast out into outer darkness. The third servant used what he was given only for himself.

The power of decision is available *now*, in the present moment. It is what happens now that shapes the life. That power is also available at our death, and what we hold in the mind and the heart at that moment shapes what follows. And so the last sentence of a prayer to Mary evokes, 'Holy Mary, Mother of God, pray for us sinners, *now and at the hour of our death.* Amen.'

We are asked to put what we have been given to good use and not hold too tightly to what we have. Jesus was asked by a wealthy man what he needed to do if he wished to follow Him (Matthew 19:16-24; Mark 10:17-25; Luke 18:18-25). Jesus told him to sell his possessions, give the money to the poor and follow Him. The man was unable to do so and Jesus said, 'It is easier for a camel to go through the eye of a needle than for a rich man to enter into the kingdom of God' (Matthew 19:24).

The key to this story is the phrase, 'the eye of a needle'. During this time walls for protection from attack or siege surrounded cities. There was a main gate or drawbridge that was closed at night. However, since travelers would often arrive after dark, there was a small entrance large enough for one man to pass through. The arched, five-foot-high entrance was called the eye of the needle. Should it happen that a late traveler with a pack animal such as a camel needed to enter the city; the animal would need to be unpacked, made to kneel, lower its head and be navigated through the narrow, low entry. To do this with an animal with the disposition of a camel was no easy matter. Hence the expression: 'More difficult than passing a camel through the eye of a needle.' This parable is not about riches. It is about humility and the willingness to kneel, lower one's head, and be separated (detached) from one's possessions so as to enter the kingdom within.

We are given reason, will, intelligence, and a role to play in the creation. We are asked to be 'the salt of the earth'. Salt was used to stop the corruption of meat and fish. We are asked to play this role in society. 'For evil to flourish all that is required is for good men to do nothing.'*

And so we are commanded to speak the truth and stand for the good. If we choose not to serve this higher purpose, then we are like 'Salt that has lost its flavor [which] is thrown into the street to be trodden under foot' (Matthew 5:13). Salt that had lost the strength to stop corruption was thrown on the walkways to melt snow and ice. If we do not serve a higher cause, we will be used to serve nature.

We are asked to be strong as Jesus was when he stood between the adulteress and the angry crowd that was about to stone her to death (John 8:3-11). With the strength of His presence and words, 'He that is without sin among you, let him first cast a stone at her.' He awakened reason, brought calm to the angry mob, evoked mercy and compassion, and when the crowd had dispersed He turned to the woman, and to His disciples, and to us all, 'Go and sin no more.'

He did not cower before the Pharisees, the Romans, His accusers, or His critics. He demonstrated the strength to remain true to oneself amidst the trials and tribulations of life, no matter how severe the storms, no matter how strong the winds, nor how high the waves; He walked upon the water (Matthew 14:22-32) and did not succumb to the storm. And when Peter stepped out of the boat to follow Him, he too walked upon the water. Then the storm raged, and Peter grew afraid and began to sink; and he called out to Jesus, who replied, 'Oh thou of little faith, wherefore didst thou doubt?' Then He cast out the doubt, and Peter rose above the water. Later remaining steadfast within Himself, the storm was abated and a calm sea restored. For the waves and turbulence are movements on the surface: the sea and His Being are deep and still. The study of the Gospels often gives rise to questions. A study group considered some frequently asked questions and offered some answers.

*Edmund Burke

QUESTION:

When Jesus found the money changers had set up tables in the temple, He upturned the tables and used a knotted rope to drive the money changers out of the temple (John 2:13-22). Were not the anger and violence a contradiction of His Teaching?

ANSWER:

Jesus did not act from anger; he did not use excessive force. He may have instilled fear or inflicted pain but there was no injury inflicted. What is being illustrated in this story is not violence but the appropriate behavior of one who knew the law and acted.

Anger implies loss of temper, loss of control, a forgetting of oneself. We know from experience that anger and loss of temper do not result in actions that are appropriate or effective. Generally actions that arise from rage have the opposite effect of what was intended. The temple was being defiled; a sacrilege was being committed. Jesus took forceful and effective action to restore the temple to its lawful purpose.

QUESTION:

In the Gospels of Mark (15:34) and Matthew (27:46) the last words of Jesus are reported as 'Eloi, Eloi, lama sabachthani?' Which has been translated, 'My God, my God, why hast thou forsaken me?', a reference to Psalm 22:1. Did Jesus forget Himself on the cross?

ANSWER:

In Luke (23:46), the last words are reported as 'Father, into thy hands I commend my Spirit'. In The Gospel of John (19:30), the last words of Jesus are, 'It is finished.'

Throughout the passion, Christ did not forget himself. He did not plead with Pilate at his trial; nor did He cry out during the torture and scourging. During his ordeal on the cross, He offered comfort to His mother and to the criminal that was being crucified next to Him. He prayed for his tormentors, 'Father, forgive them, for they know not what they do' (Luke 23:34). Jesus was sacrificed; He was not forsaken. He did not forget who and what He is. We will not be forsaken. We must strive 'to remember'. We will be asked to sacrifice. We shall be tested. There will be times when we must 'carry our cross'.

QUESTION:

Jesus commands the fig tree to bear fruit out of season (Matthew 21:19-22; Mark 11:12-14). When the tree does not, He orders it torn down and cast into the fire. Is it not unreasonable to expect the tree to bear fruit out of season?

ANSWER:

We are asked to be fruitful, speak the truth, and stand for the good. Those who do not heed the call will serve nature. We are asked to serve when the need arises; the time is not of our own choosing; service is never out of season. We are asked to serve a higher purpose, a purpose worthy of creatures created in the image of God.

QUESTION:

What is the meaning of The Holy Trinity?

ANSWER:

The unity of The Trinity – The Father, The Son, and The Holy Spirit, is a mystery beyond ordinary comprehension. God the Father is the Power of Absolute Consciousness that creates all and everything. The Son is the Consciousness of Christ – the Spirit of Universal Love, the force that sustains the creation. The Holy Spirit is the Soul or the Spiritual essence of the individual – the individual Consciousness. The Divine Mystery to be realized is that the Creative Consciousness, the Sustaining Consciousness, and the Consciousness of man are one and the same. *'The Three are One.'*

In this Work one often pauses and dedicates the moment to the Highest Good. This practice has parallels in many traditions. In the Christian tradition this dedication is expressed, 'In the name of the Father, the Son, and the Holy Spirit.'

'Amen.' (So be it.)

Note: The parables and quotes in this essay are taken from The King James Authorized Version.

Notes

CHAPTER 1

1 *Meetings with Remarkable Men*, Gurdjieff, p.36.
2 *Ibid.*, Chapter 3.
3 *Ibid.*, Chapter 7.

CHAPTER 2

1 *What Happened in Between: A Doctor's Story*, Dr William J. Welch, p.118.
2 *In Search of the Miraculous*, Ouspensky, p.262.
3 *Life is Real Only Then, When 'I Am'*, Gurdjieff, p.20.
4 *In Search of the Miraculous*, p.21.
5 *All and Everything: Beezlebub's Tales to his Grandson*, Gurdjieff, p.1219.
6 www.Gurdjieff-Legacy.org, *The Gurdjieff Journal*, 'Fourth Way Perspective' (emphasis added).
7 *It's Up to Ourselves*, Jessmin and Dushka Howarth, p.iii.
8 *In Search of the Miraculous*, p.245.
9 *What Happened in Between: A Doctor's Story*, Chapter 13.
10 *Ibid.*
11 *Ibid.*

CHAPTER 3

1 *The Bridge* #14, The Study Society, p.21.
2 *Tertium Organum*, Ouspensky, 1981 edition, p.124.
3 *In Search of the Miraculous*, quoting Gurdjieff, p.30.
4 *Ibid.* pp.124–7.
5 *It's Up to Ourselves*, p.426.
6 *In Search of the Miraculous*, p.14.
7 *A Lasting Freedom,* Dr Francis C. Roles, The Study Society, p.59; also, *The Bridge* #14, The Study Society, p.14.
8 *It's Up to Ourselves*, Chapter 7.
9 *The Bridge* #12, p.245.
10 *The Bridge* #14, p.22.
11 *Ibid.*
12 *Remembering Pyotr Demianovich Ouspensky*, a brochure written for The Centennial Collection of *The Complete Works of P.D. Ouspensky,* at the Yale Library.
13 *Ibid.*

14 The Bridge #12, p.230.
15 *Remembering Pyotr Demiaovnich Ouspensky, Ibid.*
16 *It's Up to Ourselves*, Chapter 32.
17 Transcript of 1962 conversation between Dr Roles and Shantananda Saraswati, NY Study Society.
18 Transcript of 1967 conversation with Dr Roles Preserved by the Study Society.
19 *The Bridge* #12, p.257.
20 *A Lasting Freedom*, p.59.
21 *It's Up to Ourselves*, p.497.
22 Gurdjieff Electronic Publishing, J. Walter Driscoll and George Baker, revised April 1, 1998.
23 *Ibid.*

CHAPTER 6

1 *Standing for Justice*, John Stewart, Chapter 7.

CHAPTER 7

1 'Origins of School', a lecture by Leon MacLaren, London, 1983.
2 For an account of the growth and development of the School of Economic Science see *In Search of Truth*, Brian Hodgkinson.
3 Letter from Joy Dillingham.

CHAPTER 8

1 www.buddhasanga.com/shankaraquotes
2 www.bindu.org, Govindapada's advice to Shankara, Swami Veda Bharati, May 26, 2009.

CHAPTER 9

1 *The Whole Thing, the Real Thing: Biography of Gurudeva*, p.59.
2 Brahmananda Saraswati, Wikipedia.
3 www.paulmason, Quotes of Gurudeva.
4 Translation of newspaper interview published in September 1945. www.paul mason.info/gurudev/worlswar.htm
5 *The Bridge* #12, p.244.
6 Shankaracharya Brahmananda Teachings, Oaks, NVG, Org.; also Brahmananda Saraswati, Wikiquote.

CHAPTER 10

1 *Journey of the Upanishads to the West*, Swami Tathagatananda.
2 The influence of Vedanta on philosophers in America is the subject of *American Veda*, Philipe Goldberg, Harmony Books, New York, 2010.
3 *Journey of Upanishads to the West, op. cit.*
4 www.swamisatchitananda.org/woodstock

Notes

CHAPTER 11

1 'The Promise of Peace: God's Promise and our Response', Pope John Paul II in US Bishop's Pastoral Letter.
2 *American Veda*, p.347.
3 *The Power Within*, Dorine Tolley, p.92.

CHAPTER 12

1 www.syddhayoga.org
2 *I am That*, Swami Muktananda, SYDA Foundation, pp.5-6.

CHAPTER 13

1 A Biography of Shankaracharya Shantananda Saraswati, Paul Mason. wwwpaulmason.info

CHAPTER 14

1 This quote and the facts in this chapter are taken from a transcript, kept by The Study Society, of the meeting Dr Roles had with his group in London upon returning from India in1961. The story is retold in *The Bridge* #14, pp.246-8.
2 *The Bridge* #12, p.248.
3 *The Bridge* #14, p.29.
4 The transcript of Dr Roles' meeting.
5 *Bridge* #14, pp.28-9.
6 *Bridge* #12, p.246.
7 *A Voyage of Discovery*, Dr Roles, p.ix.
8 *The Bridge* #14, p.277.
9 The transcript of Dr Roles' meeting, 1961.
10 *The Bridge* #12, p.55.
11 *Ibid.*
12 *Ibid.*
13 *Ibid.*, p.56.
14 *Ibid.*, p.57.

CHAPTER 15

1 This quote is from the 1965 conversation between Shantananda Saraswati and Leon MacLaren. The other quotes and stories of Shantananda Saraswati were from conversations between him and Dr Roles and other members of The Study Society.
2 Donald Lambie speaking to a New York group during a summer residential, approximate date 1990.
3 Adapted from a lecture given by Mr Jaiswal in London in 2006, *London Language Lectures,* School of Economic Science, 2009.
4 *The Power Within*, Dorine Tolley, p.98.
5 Related by Joy Dillingham.

6 Mr MacLaren shared this conversation with Joy Dillingham, who passed it on to the author.

7 *MacLaren Lectures*, Volume I, School of Practical Philosophy, Cape Town, p.95.

CHAPTER 16

1 *The Bridge* # 12, p.141.
2 *Conscious Unity*, Two lectures by Dr Roles, 1976.
3 *Ibid.*

CHAPTER 18

1 *The Bridge* #14, p.21.
2 *Ibid.*

Bibliography

Collin, Rodney, *The Mirror of Light*, Shambhala Publications, Inc., Boston, Mass., 1968.

Gambhirananda, Swami, *Brahma Sutra Bhasya of Shankara*, Advaita Ashrama, Calcutta, India, 1977.

George, Henry, *Progress and Poverty*, Cambridge Library Edition, Cambridge, 2009.

Goldberg, Philipe, *American Veda*, Harmony Books, New York, 2010.

Gurdjieff, G.I., *All and Everything*: *Beezlebub's Tales to his Grandson*, Dutton Publishing, New York, 1951.

Gurdjieff, G.I., *Life is Real Only Then, When 'I Am'*, Triangle Editions, New York, 1975.

Gurdjieff, G.I., *Meetings with Remarkable Men*, Viking Arcana, USA, 1991.

Hodgkinson, Brian, *In Search of Truth*, Shepheard-Walwyn, London, 2010.

Howarth, Jessmin and Dushica, *It's Up to Ourselves*, Gurdjieff Heritage Society, New York, 1998.

The King James Authorized Version, *The Bible*, Zondervan, Grand Rapids, Mich. 2002.

MacLaren, Leon, *MacLaren Lectures*, Volume I, School of Practical Philosophy, Cape Town, 1999.

Lewis, C.S., *Essays on Christianity*, HarperCollins Publishing, New York, 1980.

McIntosh, Silveig and D'Angela, Georgina, *The Bridge* #12, The Study Society, London, 1997.

McIntosh, Silveig, *The Bridge* #14, The Study Society, London, 2001.

Ouspensky, P.D., *In Search of the Miraculous: Fragments of an Unknown Teaching*, Harcourt, Inc., New York, 1949.

Ouspensky, P.D., *Tertium Organum*, third American edition, Alfred A. Knoff, New York, 1968.

Ouspensky, P.D. *The Strange Life of Ivan Osokin*, Penguin Books, Baltimore Md., 1971.

Pasricha, Prem C., *The Whole Thing the Real Thing: Biography of Gurudeva*, Delhi Photo Co., Delhi, India, 1977.

Roles, Francis C., *A Lasting Freedom*, The Society for the Study of Normal Psychology, London, 1972.

Roles, Francis C., *The Unity of Conscious Experience: Two Lectures by Dr Francis C. Roles*, The Study Society, New York, second printing, 1984.

Roles, Francis C., *Voyage of Discovery*, The Society for the Study of Human Being, New York, 1992.

Stewart, John, *Standing for Justice*, Shepheard-Walwyn, London, 2001.

Shri Purohit Swami, *The Geeta*, Faber and Faber, London, 1935.

Shri Purohit Swami and Yeats, W.B., *The Ten Principle Upanishad*, Faber and Faber, London.

Shantananda Saraswati, *Good Company: An Anthology of Sayings of Shantananda Saraswati*, The Study Society, London, 1987.

Shantananda Saraswati, *Good Company II, An Anthology of Sayings of Shantananda Saraswati*, The Study Society, London, 2010.

Shantananda Saraswati, *Teachings of His Holiness Shantananda Saraswati*, The Society for the Study of Human Being, New York, NY, 2010.

Tathagatananda, Swami, *Journey of the Upanishads to the West*, Advaita Ashrama, Kolkata, India, 2005.

Tolley, Dorine, *The Power Within*, www.createspace.com, 2008.

Welch, William J., *What Happened in Between: A Doctor's Story*, George Braziller, New York, 1972.